SIX ESSENTIALS

to Achieve

LASTING RECOVERY

Sterling T. Shumway, Ph.D., L.M.F.T.

Thomas G. Kimball, Ph.D., L.M.F.T.

HAZELDEN®

Hazelden
Center City, Minnesota 55012
hazelden.org

© 2012 by Hazelden
All rights reserved. Published 2012
Printed in the United States of America

Library of Congress Cataloging-in-Publication Data

Shumway, Sterling T.
    Six essentials to achieve lasting recovery / Sterling T. Shumway and Thomas G. Kimball.
        p. cm.
    Includes bibliographical references.
    ISBN 978-1-61649-205-2
1. Twelve-step programs. 2. Alcoholics—Rehabilitation. 3. Addicts—Rehabilitation. I. Kimball, Thomas G. II. Title.
    HV4998.S54 2012
    616.86'03—dc23

                                                        2011046486

Editor's note

Some names, details, and circumstances may have been changed to protect the privacy of those mentioned in this publication.

    This publication is not intended as a substitute for the advice of health care professionals.

    Alcoholics Anonymous, AA, and the Big Book are registered trademarks of Alcoholics Anonymous World Services, Inc.

    In chapter 4, the passage on family roles draws from Sharon Wegscheider-Cruse's *Another Chance: Hope and Health for the Alcoholic Family* (Palo Alto: Science and Behavioral Books, 1981).

16 15 14 13 12   1 2 3 4 5 6

Cover design by David Spohn
Interior design and typesetting by Kinne Design

This book is dedicated to our parents
and to the memory of
E. Widtsoe Shumway, 1927–2011.

Contents

Acknowledgments

We would like to thank our colleagues at the Center for the Study of Addiction and Recovery and at Texas Tech University in Lubbock, Texas. We are profoundly grateful to Dr. Kitty Harris, director and visionary leader of "the Center." Kitty is a great colleague and has provided an environment where the work and healing of recovery can flourish. Appreciation goes to Vince, Karen, Matt, George, and all the other faculty, staff, and students at the Center for being part of our extended family.

We recognize Don Botik and Amanda Baker at The Ranch at Dove Tree for their vision, leadership, and trust. Their support has allowed us to be innovative in the provision of multi-family services, where the principles in this book have been taught and refined. Our work with families at The Ranch has inspired our thoughts on recovery and motivated us to share these ideas. We are blessed to be part of an organization that truly cares about the treatment and recovery of the clients and families it serves.

We are indebted to the many donors who give to the Center, specifically Evelyn M. Davies and family, who funded a regents' professorship for Sterling. At a lunch meeting a few years ago, we shared the basic concept of this book with Evelyn, who encouraged us to move forward. We are also grateful to the dean of the College of Human Sciences, Dr. Linda Hoover, for her leadership and support.

Thanks to Paula D'Arcy, an accomplished author, who has inspired us on many occasions with her writing and mentoring. We appreciate her early review of the book and her encouragement to move forward.

We would like to thank our wives, Valerie and Melissa, for being the love of our lives and for their support and encouragement. We are grateful to Melissa, our first editor, for her willingness to read, edit, and give encouraging feedback regarding the manuscript. And to each of our children—we love you! To our siblings, thank you for loving us even in our weaknesses. We express deep appreciation to our parents, Widtsoe and Diane Shumway and Dale and Rachel Kimball, for being their very best when we made our worst mistakes, and for their support throughout all aspects of our lives, education, and careers.

We are grateful to the professionals at Hazelden for believing in this project and carefully walking us through the process of publishing our first book. Their patience, expertise, and guidance have meant a great deal to us.

Lastly, we are grateful for the "process" of our own friendship and the many positive "outcomes" it has generated.

. . .

Sterling would like to add a special note regarding his father, who learned that this book would be published only a few hours before his passing; thanks, Dad, for your calm example, your belief in my ideas, and your encouragement to become a writer. As noted in the book, I will forever be grateful for the "Wisdom of Widtsoe."

Introduction

Now considered an epidemic, the disease of addiction touches each of us in profound and personal ways. The individual, familial, and societal costs are staggering and are clearly understood by those who have been touched by this disease. If you are reading this book, you have probably been impacted by addiction in some way and are searching for answers or some guidance. You most likely fall within one of the following three categories:

1. You are an alcoholic/addict—or think you might be.
2. You love an addict in your role as a family member, significant other, or close friend.
3. You are a professional in the addiction/recovery field.

No matter which category you identify with, you have been affected by addiction and the far-reaching pain and consequences that result. Collectively, we the authors, Sterling and Tom, represent each of the categories listed. Personally, we understand and can empathize with the addict's plight to find recovery. We are also the family members and friends of addicts and alcoholics. Some of our loved ones found recovery, and we celebrate their lives. Others were not so fortunate. We mourn the wreckage of their lives and attend their funerals. In addition to our personal familiarity with addiction, professionally we are marriage and family therapists with extensive experience in working with addicts and their families in recovery. This book is dedicated to helping individuals and families who valiantly struggle to overcome addiction and find recovery. We use the terms "alcoholic" and "addict" interchangeably, as the same recovery principles apply to both.

The message of this book is that recovery from addiction is possible, both for addicts and for those who love them. Within these pages, you will find resources to assess and manage your recovery. This is a day-to-day journey that requires some degree of consideration regarding where you have been, where you're at currently, and where you are going. In an effort to help ourselves and others, we have identified six principles to aid in the ongoing appraisal of your "recovery walk." These principles include:

1. **Hope**
   The reawakening after despair; to expect with greater confidence.

2. **Healthy Coping Skills**
   The development of effective skills to manage the pain and stress of life.

3. **Achievement and Accomplishment**
   The movement beyond the limitations of addiction toward personal achievement.

4. **Capacity for Meaningful Relationships**
   The positive support and connection with family and peers.

5. **Unique Identity Development**
   The emergence of a unique and positive identity.

6. **Reclamation of Agency**
   The internal feeling that you have choices in your behavior—including the choice not to use (Shumway, Kimball, Dakin, Harris, and Baker, 2011).

Our discovery and understanding of these "principles of good recovery" began in discussions with individuals and families in recovery and with an exploration of the mental health and recovery research literature. We have continued to investigate these principles in our teaching, surveying, and group processing with hundreds of individuals and their family members who face the problem of addiction and find joy in their recoveries. Each of these pursuits—most importantly our own experiences and relationships with people in recovery—has taught us that those who monitor their recovery based on these specific principles become more aware and are better able to hold themselves accountable for continued growth. This personal growth includes the development of these principles such that they become the very attributes that characterize us as individuals and families in recovery. At the end of each chapter, we have added questions for you to consider that will help you to evaluate your recovery as it relates to the principles discussed in the chapter. You may want to keep a recovery journal and record your answers so you can reflect back regularly and consider your growth over time.

In many ways, you should consider the pursuit of these principles as a daily guide allowing you to ponder the strength of your recovery. This journey begins with an introduction to the principles, some thoughtful evaluation regarding their application to you, and an exploration of your progress in relation to these developing attributes. Doing these things gives you a better chance at long-term recovery, whether you identify yourself as an addict/alcoholic or as a family member. As we regularly state in our clinical work, recovery is a process of growth over time, with no punctuated final outcome—just regular, more positive successes. This journey is one of healing—a process of reclaiming what was lost—and rebuilding something better in its place. Both the journey (process) and its benefits (outcomes) are important and interconnected. Each of the attributes, from hope to meaningful relationships, and from achievement and accomplishments to healthy coping skills, should be considered from both a process and an outcome perspective:

- Gaining hope and purpose in your life is a journey, or **process,** and your ability to expect good things with greater confidence is an **outcome.**

- The **process** of learning how to cope more effectively takes time and effort, but applying these skills in a manner that cares for your recovery is an **outcome.**

- Moving away from the limits of addiction is a **process,** and achieving your aspirations and goals is an **outcome.**

- The **process** of building meaningful relationships is an ongoing effort, but the positive support and connection that occurs when these relationships are constructed is an **outcome.**

- Developing a unique identity is a life **process,** and how positive you feel about yourself today is an **outcome.**

- Reclaiming your agency to choose is a one-day-at-a-time **process** that results in greater confidence that right choices can be made, both now and in the future. This confidence is the **outcome.**

As we discuss these six principles as part of the beginning of recovery with addicts and their family members, we often ask, "What is missing from these six principles?" Most often, "spirituality" is identified as the missing component. We couldn't agree more! Although spirituality is not specifically listed as one of the principles, it is the context in which these attributes are nurtured.

One of the distinguishing features of our treatment facility in Texas is a large windmill. Practically, it serves as a landmark which identifies The Ranch at Dove Tree, an inpatient/ outpatient facility, amidst the flat and featureless West Texas landscape. Metaphorically, we see a windmill with six blades that are representative of the principles outlined in this book. These principles, or "blades," rotate around a "hub" we identify as spirituality or our relationship with our Higher Power. The hub is what holds these principles together. Additionally, within the context of spirituality, the Twelve Steps of AA serve as the foundation for our treatment approach (the base of the windmill).

Upon graduation from outpatient treatment, individuals are given a metal placard in the form of the sun, with the word "spirit" stamped in clay in the middle. This idea, developed by Dr. Kitty Harris and designed by Vince Sanchez at the Center for the Study of Addiction and Recovery, Texas Tech University, symbolizes the "sunlight of the spirit" discussed in the Big Book of Alcoholics Anonymous (2002). Applying these six principles to your recovery and remembering their spiritual context will help you to maintain your walk and enjoy the "sunlight of the spirit" along the way. This personal and spiritual progression is a journey from resentment and unhappiness to healing and peace. This walk allows you to grow in ways you never thought possible and to become the person you were meant to be. As you embrace the sunlight through your relationship with your Higher Power, you will live each day with honesty and integrity and be more willing to acknowledge your weaknesses. With humility you will make amends and begin to reach out for help through meaningful relationships. Discovering the sunlight is part of your spiritual journey, your search to find the purpose and meaning of your life. For many people, this placard represents reaching a place in their recovery where, even in their darkest hour, they realize sunlight is not far away. For us, this defines the process of recovery.

As a way of embracing the spiritual context found in the Twelve Steps and in these six principles of good recovery, we have written a recovery prayer. This prayer will help you to remember these principles and actively use them in your daily meditations. Regular affirmations such as prayer will help you internalize these principles in a manner where they become resources that can be used to sustain your recovery. The prayer is as follows:

God, thank you for the chance at recovery.

Grant me **hope** and transform me into a new person who can **cope** more effectively.

Help me recognize the **accomplishments** in my life and develop a greater **capacity for meaningful relationships.**

As I emerge anew, **change my identity** to one more positive and allow me to reclaim my **agency** by always choosing recovery.

Amen.

Hope

A REAWAKENING AFTER DESPAIR;
TO EXPECT WITH GREATER CONFIDENCE

We define hope as "a reawakening after despair" and "to expect with greater confidence." The spiral of addiction creates despair. When you hit bottom and realize there is no hope without change—only more destruction and ultimately death—a reawakening occurs. Hitting bottom is often called a moment of clarity, a moment of grace, or a moment of hope. It is a moment of clarity when you grasp that the pain and despair of addiction exceed any benefit of using. Hope emerges when you become aware that living is an option. For those of you who have fallen off the edge and have found the cold, hard bottom of addiction—short of dying—you realize there is nowhere to go but up.

This bottom is the beginning of a new set of expectations, the most important of which is the realization that failure and ultimately death (emotional, spiritual, psychological, and physical) doesn't have to be your destiny. This fall provides the initial springboard to a renewal of hope and to a greater faith. This is where you begin to understand not just "who you are" (a moment of clarity) but "who you can become" (a lifetime of clarity). In contrast to the pain and despair of addiction, this hope—within a spiritual context—is transformative. It allows you to find your identity, develop meaningful relationships, achieve and accomplish, cope in more effective ways, and reclaim your agency by making better choices.

> In a moment of clarity you see who you are—
> in the moments that follow, you begin to
> understand who you can become.
>
> — STERLING T. SHUMWAY

...

Part of what has inspired our conception of hope is what addicts and family members have shared with us related to their recovery, as well as their personal definitions of hope. As you read some of these examples, think about your own journey and consider how these fit within your own definition of hope.

"Hope is believing that maybe, just maybe, it can get better."

"Hope is breathing again and believing in the possibilities."

"Hope is finding a reason to go on or keep hanging on."

"Hope is freedom from bondage."

"Hope is finding those things to look forward to."

"Hope is a belief in the future."

As you can see, these are powerful definitions that helped us to formulate our conception of hope—that is, the reawakening after despair; to expect with greater confidence. This reawakening includes the belief that life is good and there is freedom from the bondage of addiction. To expect with greater confidence includes the assurance that there are a multitude of possibilities in your future. Because of these possibilities, there are reasons to move forward and hang on when life gets difficult or produces pain. Interestingly, most of these hope definitions came from addicts and family members early in their recovery.

According to the First Step of a Twelve Step perspective, you must admit that you are powerless over alcohol (or whatever addiction might beset you) and that your life has become unmanageable. This often results from reaching the cold, hard bottom spoken of earlier. Your emerging humility makes it more likely to accomplish the Steps that follow, Steps Two and Three. Step Two requires you to believe in a Higher Power that is greater than you and can restore you to sanity. Further, Step Three says that this understanding allows you to make the decision to turn your will and life over to the care of the God of your understanding. We believe that these first three Steps are as important for family members and those who love addicts as they are for the addicts themselves. They provide a level of common ground and dialogue for families to discuss and traverse their recoveries. Perhaps more importantly, the exchange articulated below is a necessary outcome for both addict and family member.

While working these Steps, there is an exchange that occurs between you and your Higher Power. This exchange requires some giving and some getting, characteristics of a "reciprocal relationship." Often, those struggling with addiction are unfamiliar with this give-and-take type of relationship. Rather than being a two-way street (reciprocal), relationships where addiction is present become a one-way train wreck where selfishness and isolation are primary.

Through these first three Steps, you establish a foundation in conjunction with your Higher Power. On a spiritual level, you are linking to a conduit of hope, something greater than yourself. Without this linkage, without the connection to this conduit, you are left on your own, and fear and despair may overtake you again. Fear plays the negative messages of the past over and over in your mind—messages such as "You can't do anything right," "You've wasted your life" or "You've ruined everybody else's life," and "You can't be forgiven." These negative messages based in fear often combine to create one large message: "You are worthless."

Eliminating the fear marks the beginning of the process of healing. Making this connection with your Higher Power takes the greatest act of humility—the surrendering of your will and your life. This is a decision to extend the moment of clarity to something more lasting. We cultivate this clarity and hope the same way we learn to walk: one step at a time, one moment at a time, one day at a time! There is an additional exchange that occurs in this conduit of hope (the exchange between you and your Higher Power), where you trade pride for humility, fear

The Twelve Steps of Alcoholics Anonymous

1. We admitted we were powerless over alcohol—that our lives had become unmanageable.

2. Came to believe that a Power greater than ourselves could restore us to sanity.

3. Made a decision to turn our will and our lives over to the care of God *as we understood Him.*

4. Made a searching and fearless moral inventory of ourselves.

5. Admitted to God, to ourselves, and to another human being the exact nature of our wrongs.

6. Were entirely ready to have God remove all these defects of character.

7. Humbly asked Him to remove our shortcomings.

8. Made a list of all persons we had harmed, and became willing to make amends to them all.

9. Made direct amends to such people wherever possible, except when to do so would injure them or others.

10. Continued to take personal inventory and when we were wrong promptly admitted it.

11. Sought through prayer and meditation to improve our conscious contact with God *as we understood Him,* praying only for knowledge of His will for us and the power to carry that out.

12. Having had a spiritual awakening as the result of these steps, we tried to carry this message to alcoholics, and to practice these principles in all our affairs.

The Twelve Steps of AA are taken from *Alcoholics Anonymous,* 4th ed., published by AA World Services, Inc., New York, NY, 59–60.

for faith, and despair for hope. The benefits of this exchange are that the negative messages begin to fade and are replaced with more positive affirmations such as "I am a good person and can make things right" and "I can be forgiven and am capable of forgiving others."

An illustration of overcoming fear, connecting with the God of your understanding through this conduit of hope, and finding peace and acceptance is illustrated in the following story as shared by Tom.

🍃 Several years ago during Christmas time, our third child and second son, Nathaniel (a.k.a. Big Nato), then three years old, became very ill. We were nervous because even with medical help, he wasn't getting better. As moms often do, my wife Melissa "knew" something was really wrong with our son. She pushed the doctors to look closer at our situation. A couple of days later, after consulting with more medical professionals, we found ourselves sitting in the middle of the pediatric intensive care unit of our local hospital. A pediatric oncologist informed us that our son most likely had acute lymphoblastic leukemia, a form of childhood cancer. In that moment, the foundation of our world began to crumble. This foundation fully collapsed when his cancer diagnosis was confirmed a few days later. I felt as if a train ran right over me. And then, as if the train engineer wasn't satisfied with his initial attempt, just for good measure he backed up and ran over my entire family again.

Following the doctor's diagnosis, I remember staying up nights and praying to God that my son would live. I felt my world spinning out of control and wasn't sure how to proceed. I was terrified for Big Nato and our young family, which included three other children. Early in the process, Melissa confided in me that sometimes she was resentful of the sun itself, as if its rise and fall mocked her each day. She felt that the world should stop, pay attention, and take notice that her son was sick and our family was hurting. But the world didn't stop and the sun continued to rise day after day. It was a relief to have someone else understand how I felt. As we moved forward with the initial treatment, powerful dark clouds of despair quickly developed and dumped torrential rain over me. Flash floods of disheartenment washed away my stores of energy and hope.

In my greatest despair, it was my friend in recovery, Sterling, who stood by me, offering direction and guidance through the storm. In a hospital room adjacent to my son's, we prayed together one afternoon early in my son's treatment. My friend entreated his Higher Power on my behalf that I would find peace and hope. I heard him humbly petition God and ask that once I found my own hope, that God would allow me to become a life preserver, a safety vest, to my wife and my children. It was an impressive prayer from a man who understood pain and sorrow and the fruits of recovery. In that moment, the sunlight of hope began to shine through and dispel the torrential rain. I found myself holding on to a conduit of hope, beyond my own self. This conduit of hope offered me strength to make it through the day. An exchange occurred between my Higher Power and me where I began to give up my desire to control the outcome of my son's disease by offering my will to God in exchange for His unconditional love.

My initial effort to reach out for help fostered a continued effort to reach out to others, including family and friends.

In an attempt to more fully understand the disease we faced, I had a particularly important conversation with our oncologist, Dr. Melanie Oblender. Sitting with her, I mustered my courage and reached out for her help. I asked her, "How did my son get cancer?" This question was a loaded and selfish one. What I really wanted to know was, "What did I do wrong?" and "Is my son's cancer my fault?"—negative messages that haunted me and are often what occur in moments of significant pain. After trying to explain the multiple factors that are part of the development of any disease, including addiction (e.g., genetic, environmental, and psychological), she said something I will always remember. As if sensing my real question, she said, "Tom, it really doesn't matter how your son got cancer. All that truly matters now is his treatment and recovery from the disease." In my head I knew she was right. But most importantly, this conversation helped me hear my Higher Power say to my heart, "Tom, throw the shame and blame out the window."

Later I asked her a second question: "What are the chances my son will survive?" She looked at me thoughtfully and said something that changed my life and our prospects in recovery. She said, "It will be 0 or 100 percent for your boy, so let's focus on the 100 percent." In essence, she was telling me either Nato would make it or he wouldn't—it didn't really matter what the prognosis for anyone else was. I have thought many times about this statement and how it relates to addiction, recovery, and relapse. When family members and addicts approach me and ask about relapse rates and survival percentages from the disease of addiction, I share Dr. Oblender's wisdom. For you and your family, you will either be successful in recovery or you won't—no one else's journey in recovery matters. In my own journey, after these conversations with Dr. Oblender, I tried harder not to blame myself or become consumed with "the chances" of failure, so that I might better focus on my own needs and the needs of my family.

As things often go, life continued to be a struggle for Nato and our entire family. It was as if when Nato contracted cancer, we all got sick. Again, this reminded me of addiction, where whole families are impacted by the disease of one of its members. As a matter of necessity, in the months that followed, Melissa and I split the care of Nato and our other children. We made a rule that one of us would spend twenty-four hours at the hospital and the other at home, or at work, and then switch. Although family and friends helped, we were like those "ships that pass in the night"— it was incredibly difficult. Nato's health required that we spend almost all of the first five months of his treatment in the hospital.

During this time, it seemed to me that everything turned against us. We would finally get him released from the hospital, and then he would spike a fever and have to go right back in. He was close to death several times. When my son was four years old, I remember him asking me, "Dad, am I going to die?" With no good answer to his question, I did my best to comfort him and said, "Not today, Big Nato, not today."

Over the long months, I watched Nato's disease take a

tremendous toll on all of us. My initial grasp on hope and connection with my Higher Power slowly faded. One day, after finally getting Nato home and returning to work, I remember receiving a call from Melissa informing me through her tears that Nato had once again spiked a fever. I told her I would meet her at the hospital and hung up the phone.

Months of grief, pain, despair, and anger rushed over me. My feelings were intense. As I drove, I directed all of my anguish at God with accusing and undignified expressions of anger. I cursed and swore and said things to Him that to this day make me cringe. It was in this, my worst moment, that I had a remarkable experience. I can only describe it as God, with His unconditional love, coming into my car and wrapping His arms around me. All of my negative emotions faded in an instant, and all I could feel was love. Tears flowed and I wept. In my mind, God spoke and said two powerful words: "Trust me." After months of struggle, I truly understood the exchange my Higher Power was trying to make with me. It was so simple, yet incredibly difficult. I finally was able to give my will over to my Higher Power and trust Him with everything, including my son's life. In return, He gave me His amazing love, a message of trust, and the knowledge that I would be OK whether my son lived or died.

You should know that Tom regularly shares this story with addicts and family members as a way to develop common ground. As with Tom's son's disease, they know what it is like to feel totally out of control and to pray to their Higher Power to save themselves or their loved one. They, like Tom's family, know that when one family member gets sick, everyone gets sick. Diseases such as cancer and addiction spread through relationships like a wildfire, wreaking havoc on everyone. Fathers, mothers, husbands, wives, and significant others blame themselves and ask the question, "What did I do wrong that my loved one has this disease?"

Dr. Oblender's advice to Tom in his moment of need is just as applicable to you who are reading this book. Trying to figure out who is to blame for your addiction or your loved one's disease is fruitless. It truly doesn't matter now. You need to focus on treatment and/or recovery and finally throw blame and shame out the window. In addition, don't compare your recovery or the chances of success or failure to others. Focus on 100 percent recovery for you and your loved ones. Most importantly, let us assure you that your Higher Power's conduit of hope will open and sustain you if you just reach out and turn your will over to the God of your understanding, whether you are an addict or someone who loves an addict.

In relation to addiction, part of the benefit of maintaining your recovery through this conduit of hope is seeing the possibility of being right with God. In this relationship, you must give over your illusion of control (based in fear) to get something back in return. What you get is forgiveness of self and a release of your unrealistic expectations. You experience an unconditional acceptance and love that may have previously been a foreign concept to you. The receiving of your Higher Power's love is the first step on your journey of self-forgiveness—of learning how to first tolerate and then accept your imperfections. On this voyage you will learn not only how to forgive yourself but also how to accept forgiveness from your Higher Power and others. With this renewed hope comes trust, and with this trust you can begin to extend similar forgiveness to others. Without this forgiveness from God, from yourself, and for others, true hope evades you. Being right with God, ourselves, and others is the outcome of hope. With hope, you believe that, in conjunction with your Higher Power, you can accomplish anything.

Hope is contagious and begins to permeate all of your social and personal interactions. One of the negative by-products of addiction is the trail of "dead" relationships that are left behind. Some of these associations may need to remain in the "dead" category for your success in recovery. However, hope tells us that there are relationships that can and should be revived. As is the case in a flower garden, many plants and flowers go dormant during the cold winter months. Some plants appear to be dead and others exist only below the garden's surface—deep within the soil. With the advent of greater sunlight and warmth, water, and nutrients, these plants and flowers are revitalized and spring forth into a beautiful chorus of colors. Like sun to the flower, hope offers warmth and light to the soul and to the souls around us. The person in recovery who attends to the soil and spends time in the recovery garden nurturing these relationships (the process) can expect good things, such as the blossoming of meaningful relationships (the outcome).

Hope also provides the water and nutrients to resurrect relationships thought to be dead and to cause other critical relationships to spring forth and grow into recovery support systems. Like many relationships bruised by addiction, some bulbs and flowers lie dormant. After proper care, sunlight, and nutrients (akin to taking care of your own recovery, making amends, and staying clean/sober), these dormant relationships may emerge and blossom. Just as we cannot make flowers grow without the flowers' cooperation, these relationships cannot be forced, only fostered and encouraged. Some relationships will not respond to the care and will need to be allowed to lie dormant.

With hope in your heart, you will stay in the present—not beating yourself up for the relationship wreckage of the past. We often inflict unnecessary pain on ourselves when we dwell only on our mistakes, immersing ourselves in the anxiety of previous failures or attempting to obsessively control our futures. These anxieties and attempts at control go contrary to the one-day-at-a-time perspective so important to healthy recovery. As a guide in our relationships, hope mentors patience and acceptance of how things are, not how we want them to be. Within this new space, bruised relationships are rebuilt and begin to grow and flourish. Other relationships should be discarded if they cannot coexist within a recovery context.

Recovery is a greenhouse of sorts. What grows within it should be nurtured and cared for, and what doesn't should be allowed to die.

Perhaps most difficult for any gardener are flowers that have died and will never emerge again. Particularly early in recovery, some relationships must be severed. Other relationships will slowly die if given unrealistic expectations and demands. Change creates dissonance in relationships, especially when others are not in sync with these changes. Addiction has the potential to kill even the strongest friendships and familial ties—the trauma, abuse, and neglect caused by addiction extract a terrible toll. The lies, infidelity, financial ruin, manipulation, and control are all part of the addiction spiral and are never victimless.

Hope can only burn bright if you are not constantly subjecting yourself to the pain of past relationships and to the loud call of those who don't want you to change. Those persons you love who are not in recovery may say things such as, "You're not really an addict—just come and be with us," or "You don't have to use—just one more for old times' sake." Further still, old friends may say, "You can't make it without us; we are the only friends you have." The thought of these dead relationships can be devastatingly overwhelming, but remember that acceptance of these dead relationships is part of good recovery. In the beginning, you may find yourself standing with your Higher Power as your only friend, but know that this is enough in the critical moments of early recovery and will change over time.

We want you, the reader, to know that we understand the pain of severing long-term relationships. In an effort to keep the voices of the past from sabotaging him, Sterling, early on in his recovery, chose to end important friend and girlfriend relationships. This choice allowed the roots of early recovery to be established and, subsequently, allowed many flowers to bloom. Such a task took one evening of pain and many days of boundary setting to ensure decades of amazing recovery. According to Sterling:

> Severing these relationships was probably the hardest and most important thing I did to establish and protect my recovery. Though there was guilt associated with these important boundaries, I continued to hold the line, knowing that if I didn't it would only be a matter of time before I was with old friends and engaging in old behaviors. For a time, it was only my Higher Power, my parents, and me. It was a significant change, but it was necessary.

Your connection with your Higher Power, and the conduit of hope that naturally flows from this reciprocal relationship, are the vehicles that will help you draw good boundaries and form new relationships. As was the case with Sterling, this connection will also help you heal the pain and protect you from the lies embedded in feelings of guilt and shame. Hope encourages you to move forward knowing that peace and healing lie ahead.

Be aware that early recovery may be fraught with other trapdoors and difficulties—something we refer to as "hope killers." Hope is difficult to hold on to when you are experiencing pain. In addition to the pain of relationships lost, there are other sources of pain that must be addressed if you are going to nurture this garden of recovery. These include the pain of imperfection, trauma, depression, anxiety, and other mental health issues or concerns (e.g., attention deficit disorder, attention deficit/hyperactivity disorder, bipolar disorder, personality disorders). The presence of an addiction and one of these other pain-producing concerns is referred to as a dual or co-occurring disorder.

A mental health issue can severely complicate recovery and must be properly treated. It is estimated that one out of every two people who struggle with addiction also have a mental health disorder. These mental health issues should be dealt with medically and therapeutically, and include the consideration of medication. Our experience is that addicts and their family members are often reluctant to take appropriate and prescribed treatments for these concerns. Though care should be given and professional advice sought from professionals experienced in addiction and recovery, medication should be an option. Properly medicated, most of the pain of depression and/or anxiety (or, for that matter, any other diagnosable mental health issue) may subside. A parallel example would be someone who suffers from migraine headaches, high cholesterol, or diabetes looking for relief without the proper medication. We recognize that behavioral and/or life changes are essential, but those alone may not be enough.

In addition, trauma, whether experienced early in childhood or later in life, is often another pain that addicts and their family members carry into recovery—another "hope killer." The emotional and psychological pain of trauma will tempt you to cope in old and unhealthy ways. Recovery from your trauma is as important as recovery from your addiction. In your focus to find healing, have the courage to talk with a safe person openly and honestly about your trauma. Despite the difficulty of sharing it at first, you must deal with it as part of your recovery or you will pay the price later. Remember, when overwhelmed by the past, relapse is always a possibility. Dealing with it now—in a hopeful, healthy, and therapeutic way—provides the resources to handle the regular pains of life that will surely emerge, without your being overwhelmed by the combination of the two.

Considerations of Hope

This section is designed to help you think through and apply the concepts addressed in this chapter. As you contemplate and consider the hope in your life, remember that obtaining hope is a process or journey with both immediate and long-term outcomes. Addicts and family members should consider how these ideas relate specifically to them and their recovery, avoiding the temptation to apply these principles to others. Remember that recovery is for all who suffer from addiction. Giving our will over to our Higher Power and finding hope is as important for the family member as it is for the addict. The first three Steps are a wonderful place for addicts and family members to find common ground.

With the knowledge that most individuals and families experience the spiral of addiction and hit bottom, consider the following questions:

- What has the spiral of addiction been like for you?

- Have you realized that the pain and despair of addiction has exceeded the benefits of using or enabling? When you realized this, what did you do next?

- How does it feel to know that living free from your addiction or the pains of addiction is an option?

- Who are you now? Who or what can you become in your recovery?

In this chapter, we defined hope in several ways. Hope is a very personal concept. Ask yourself, "What is my definition of hope?"

- What are those things, both internal and external, that cause you to feel hopeful?

- Is the God of your understanding part of that equation?

- How can you make your Higher Power part of your recovery?

Consider discussing with someone you respect how they hold on to hope, even when life gets difficult (these are the people that seem to have mastered what you are striving for).

Have you been introduced to the Twelve Steps of Alcoholics Anonymous, Narcotics Anonymous, or another appropriate Twelve Step program? If you are not familiar with these Steps, we encourage you to seek them out and become familiar with them. If you already have, then consider the following:

- What have you learned from working the first three Steps?

- Have you considered what the process might be like to give your will over to the care of your Higher Power? Do you have the necessary humility to accomplish this?

- What would it be like to connect to a conduit of hope and have a truly reciprocal relationship with your Higher Power or someone else that you love?

- What would it be like to believe that you can be forgiven by your Higher Power, yourself, and others?

As stated earlier, addiction is fraught with negative messages. List the negative messages you carry around in your head and heart about yourself.

- With hope as your guide, what new messages should you believe as part of your recovery?

- Think about and then visualize what it would be like to be a "good person capable of great things."

- How does it feel to know that you can make things right?

We believe that Dr. Oblender's wisdom and advice to Tom and his family, while they faced the disease of cancer with their son and brother, has relevance to you in your recovery journey.

- How do you learn to throw the blame and shame of addiction out the window?

- How would your life be different if you focused on your recovery in the present and stopped trying to figure out the "whys" of the past?

- How much stress and anxiety could you eliminate in your life if you could turn over some of the specifics of your future to your Higher Power?

- What difference would it make if you stopped comparing yourself to others?

- What difference would it make if you stopped comparing your chances of success to the chances of others?

- What would it look like if you focused 100 percent on your own recovery?

In this chapter, we likened recovery to a garden, with you as the gardener.

- How can you make your recovery garden grow?

- What does the sunlight of recovery mean to you?

- What relationships do you need to say good-bye to so that your recovery garden can flourish?

- What relationships do you need to nurture?

- How can a connection with a conduit of hope, your Higher Power, help you stay strong in your recovery and form new and supportive relationships?

There are many pitfalls of early recovery that must be identified and dealt with. In this chapter we refer to them as "hope killers."

- List the "killers" of your hope.
- List the pitfalls you need to be mindful of in your recovery.
- How can your Higher Power help you avoid and manage these "killers" of hope?

Do you suffer from addiction and another mental health disorder such as anxiety, depression, or bipolar disorder, for example? Suffering from two disorders is very common for addicts and alcoholics.

- Are you getting the help you need to address both issues?
- Are you reluctant to take medication even when appropriate professionals are advocating the need for it?
- If recommended, consider the benefit of taking proper medication as you make appropriate behavioral changes.

Many addicts and their family members also are sufferers of trauma and must carry both the pain of addiction and their trauma into their recovery.

- Is someone you are currently in a relationship with being physically, sexually, or emotionally abusive to you? Have you suffered these traumas in the past and dealt with them appropriately?

- Are there people in your life who do not respect your boundaries?

- Have you considered reaching out for help to persons who can support you in a therapeutic way?

- How does talking about and healing from traumas help you in your recovery?

• • •

The list of statements that follows can assist you in evaluating your level of hope in an effort to manage your recovery. As you consider your hope in the context of these statements, keep in mind that recovery is a day-to-day journey. Finding and holding on to hope is an ongoing process and part of the journey. As you think about and work on your connection with your Higher Power, you should see the benefits and outcomes of having more hope in your life. Use these statements to regularly assess your level of hope in relation to your recovery.

On the scale provided, assess your level of hope
based on the following statements:

1	2	3	4	5
Very Low Hope	Low Hope	Middle Hope	High Hope	Very High Hope

The future appears bright to me.   _____

I have a reason for living.   _____

Things in my life are looking up.   _____

I am optimistic about my future.   _____

I see the purpose of my life.   _____

I am feeling more positive.   _____

▶ If your pattern of answers falls in the middle to high end of the hope continuum, then you are on the right track for today.

▶ If you find yourself falling into the middle to low end of the scale, either you are early in recovery and still learning, or you are struggling and need to reach out for help.

Healthy Coping Skills

THE DEVELOPMENT OF EFFECTIVE SKILLS TO MANAGE THE PAIN AND STRESS OF LIFE

Learning to cope in a more healthy way is where all the theories and process discussions about addiction and recovery are applied on a practical level. This is where the "pedal hits the metal" or "the rubber meets the road." Recovery cannot be done while residing in the cheap seats. It takes hard work, changes in behavior, resolve, long-term effort, faith, and renewed relationships. Each requires you to be an active participant in the process of recovery. We know for certain that unless you find better ways to cope, you will soon be using again or engaging in other addictive behaviors.

As with any other resolutions or goals you may have made in your life, coping skills will develop only through the efforts listed above and with the help of others. Resolutions—as is the case with recovery—are best done with the help and support of other people. Good recovery is accomplished by teaming up with another person (or persons) who understands, so you can hold each other accountable. This person should be a "key person," defined as someone who can be trusted, who understands the process of addiction, and who is educated and supportive of your recovery.

Coping is an internal and an external process, an inside and an outside job. Both the inside and the outside portions of coping are ultimately your responsibility to direct, but can be aided by the presence of those key persons. The inside job begins with the metamorphosis that occurs when you embrace the first three Steps of recovery and find hope in your life. It is the beginning of a new way of feeling, a new way of thinking, and a new way of acting. What happens in the early stages of this inside job is that you have a spiritual awakening that provides you the energy to begin coping differently. At the most basic level, this is a decision to begin reaching out to others—to your Higher Power, professional help, family, and friends. Reaching out for help is the first of the coping skills you learn in recovery and should be practiced throughout. This reaching out is the beginning of the inside coordinating with the outside and the start of making you accountable for better choices.

All of these changes can be facilitated in a more effective manner with the help of family, friends, sponsors, Twelve Step groups, counselors, and so on. These relationships are the external resources that help to support and maintain the internal changes. These changes, if made thoughtfully and with support, are the beginnings of new and healthier ways to cope. Hopefully you can see the intertwining relationship between the internal and the external, and the synergy that can be created by focusing on both. Successful recovery will depend on the staying power of these decisions and choices and their long-term sustainability.

When we turn our will over to the God of our understanding, it can help us cope more effectively. Our Higher Power teaches us to seek wisdom and strength from others who tutor us and encourage us in our new ways of feeling, thinking, and acting. There is a transaction that occurs between us and those we reach out to that reflects how God works with us. As stated in chapter 1, there is an exchange that occurs—our will and humility for others' grace and help. This is the coaching/mentoring we need to change our behaviors over the long term and to find lasting solutions to old pain and problems. With time, as trust in our relationships builds, we become more open to new ways of coping and to more effective strategies for maintaining recovery. Trust must grow before we will allow ourselves to be held accountable by anyone. In our addiction, we experienced little trust, some paranoia, and monumental stubbornness—all supported by the denial of addiction.

As you learn to trust, remember that people aren't always as dependable as you might like them to be; as a result, a little trial and error must be allowed to occur without blaming yourself for others' inability to provide support. Not everything is your fault. However, if a lack of support becomes a pattern, you may need to let go and look for others who are more capable of watching your back. Make no mistake that recovery is an interpersonal process that may require the exclusion of some and the inclusion of others (discussed in chapter 1). Being open to who needs to go and who needs to stay is extremely important as a healthy coping skill. Setting boundaries is not always an easy task, but it is necessary. The act of putting a wide boundary between us and those who may not be able to be helpful, and between us and those who would entice us to cope in old ways, is critical and necessary in good recovery.

Before we can truly trust others, we must learn to trust ourselves—this is a by-product of finding forgiveness. If nothing else, we can begin to trust that we are worthy of help from others, and that unconditional support can always be counted on from our Higher Power and from key persons in our lives. Forgiveness of self is another different and healthy way to cope. You need to find redemption so you don't feel the constant shame of past, present, and expected future failures. When we connect with our Higher Power and make amends, our level of shame drops below our level of ability to cope, meaning our coping resources exceed our pain. If our coping level exceeds our level of pain and shame, we can better look after our recovery. If our pain and shame exceed our level of coping resources, we become vulnerable in recovery and move further away from our Higher Power. This pain and shame keep us from having a relationship with God and receiving the needed resources that come from such an interaction.

When we begin moving beyond the first three Steps, we find even greater acceptance and redemption from those around us involved in our recovery. We realize that others can accept us for who we are, and we cleanse our soul by acknowledging the exact nature of our wrongs, speaking them out loud, and making amends. Remember, there is nothing healthy about being ashamed about the past. Shame is a personal attack on you as a person. It is not healthy sorrow for mistakes made. Engaging in amends is a powerful intervention that leads to more active coping skills spurred by taking a healthy inventory of your life and experiencing the subsequent sorrow that follows. This is normal—having sorrow as opposed to shame.

You must also make sure that you are not being subverted in your progress by other less helpful partnerships such as family-of-origin pain, depression/anxiety, or any other physical/mental disorder. These partnerships never encourage, never give hope or faith; instead they tell you that you can't make it—so why even try. This is the number one enemy of developing long-lasting coping skills: the thunderous remnants of old ways rooted deep in the mind and soul that tell you that you are inept, inadequate, unable to hold the line, and certainly not worthy of the good things in life. These old remnants make bad accountability partners because they judge you based on old markers that will always make you feel inadequate and not up to the task. These are hope killers!

To overcome the remnants of the past and root out these negative voices, you must begin managing your "shame" differently. As mentioned, there is a difference between shame and healthy sorrow. Healthy sorrow for past mistakes creates a dissonance that provides the motivation to change things in your life. Shame, however, causes you to turn the dissonance in on yourself and equate it with being a bad person, rather than a person who behaves badly. These are two very different things. Healthy sorrow will spur you to change; shame will keep you from making any changes at all. Shame provides a constant negative commentary on your thoughts, your actions, and your life. Managing shame is a lifetime process and is made easier by the key persons in your life who can model unconditional love and support despite your imperfections. You can't manage on a convenience basis (a little here and a little there) and get results; you must be vigilant and pay attention, going back to the first three Steps when your worth and value need reinforcement.

Sterling tells the story of his father's counsel, given to him early in his recovery. He credits his father's guidance as important in maintaining healthy coping skills and keeping him close to his Higher Power. He writes:

> 🖋 At an important transition point in my life, I sought my father's wisdom and counsel. I remember him leaning over his desk saying, "Son, you're going to make mistakes in your life—don't let these mistakes keep you away from God and cause you to fall out of the game!" He said further, "Many people let the shame and guilt of their mistakes keep them from the very places and people they should be associating with." Though I didn't understand the value of my father's advice at that time, I have pondered his words at critical moments since and have benefited from their wisdom—the "Wisdom of Widtsoe" as I used to call it, since my father's name was Widtsoe.

These simple but powerful words have kept me in the game of life, and more importantly have beckoned me to keep going forward, even in times it would have been easier to quit. When mistakes are made, I have been able to set them aside and not exclude myself from the love of my God, the company of my family, and the pursuit of my faith. I have not let guilt and shame win the battle for my attention, my time, or my soul. I feel sorry when mistakes are made, but, remembering my father's advice, I don't allow shame to be part of the equation. I keep moving forward. 🖋

If you are an addict or family member in recovery, these should be powerful words to your ears. How many times have you counted yourself out because you did not feel worthy, felt ashamed, or somehow felt you didn't deserve the bounties of life? How often have you let your negative feelings about yourself determine your choices, your future plans, or your relationship with your Higher Power? Taking Sterling's father's advice by "staying in the game" is a different way of coping, a different way of thinking, a different way of doing! It requires a moment-by-moment, one-day-at-a-time effort.

Another helpful way to cope is by changing your recovery temperature, a process we believe begins at the outset of recovery. Upon entering treatment or making a commitment to sobriety, you will find a number of people who are not on the same page as you, or who appear to be running (metaphorically) at a different temperature. These are people who have not yet embraced recovery and may include family members and friends. It is possible these family members and friends are those who may have contributed to your problem. They are those you felt comfortable with in your addiction because they ran the same temperature you did. Some of you can certainly remember entering into a treatment facility or recovery support group and feeling completely out of place. Our guess is that you were running hot while other recovering addicts already had some time to cool off. This is what happens in treatment and recovery; we slowly but surely shift our temperature to a more healthy level. As our temperature changes, we change our level of understanding and perception. The longer you are in treatment/recovery, the more comfortable you feel. With time, your temperature shifts to match those recovering persons surrounding you.

Consider the difference you felt when you walked back out into the real world and began rubbing shoulders with your previous peer groups or family members who had not embraced recovery. Was there a temperature differential? Yes, of course! Was it all warm and fuzzy as you all expressed similar goals and attitudes? No, of course not! Without a cadre of supportive people around you who burn at a similar recovery temperature, you may slip back into a place of addiction where the majority temperature will rule. This is where those "key persons" become absolutely essential. They have the same recovery temperature as you and can provide insulation for your recovery.

Just like this temperature shift, change in recovery is necessary. There is a systems theory term called "homeostasis" that helps explain our resistance to change and our tendency to slip into old ways of coping. This word as we describe it in our treatment groups is defined as "non-change." Coping differently takes energy. The homeostatic forces (non-change forces) push against you, attempting to maintain the status quo and limiting your ability to change. These homeostatic forces provide a degree of stress and pressure for the person in recovery and permeate his or her interactions with friends and family. Often these non-change forces can be seen when people make big changes in their lives—for example, changing their faith or their using status. Just watch how everyone marshalls the forces of non-change to prevent the person from making the changes. Anger and manipulation may be employed to maintain the status quo.

When relational stress closes in and we become rigid and fearful about our recovery, it becomes hard to cope in a proactive way, and we are forced to become more reactive (the old way of coping). Managing these stressors, both inside and out, needs to be a significant part of your recovery and will lead to better coping. This stress is like the other co-occurring factors that can bring you down and create the pain that always tempts you to artificially cope—to maintain your temperature at a using level. To learn to cope more effectively, you must manage the stressors in your life more effectively. It is always easier when someone is there to support you, push you, and encourage you toward positive change.

To learn to deal with the stressors in your life more effectively, think about the following considerations. They fall into three categories: (1) managing yourself better, (2) managing your reaction to stress better, and (3) managing the amount of pain and stress in your life. Consider these specifics for coping differently in each of these areas.

1. Managing yourself
   - Acknowledge your own worth
   - Exercise and eat right to stay healthy
   - Get enough rest and sleep
   - Learn to enjoy life without using
   - Find a hobby
   - Improve communication skills
   - Improve conflict resolution skills
   - Increase your spiritual enrichment

2. Managing your reaction to stress
   - Don't be stressed about the things you can't change
   - Change your self-talk
   - Avoid overreacting
   - Find the humor in life
   - Learn to expect and enjoy the unexpected
   - Allow yourself a time-out
   - Learn how to relax through imagery and meditation

3. Managing the amount of stress
   - Be realistic with your expectations
   - Practice good time management

- Take life one day at a time
- Don't sweat the small stuff
- Learn to set boundaries and to say no
- Manage your money and other daily obligations more realistically

In order to manage ourselves, our reaction to stress, and the amount of stress in our lives, we must establish healthy boundaries—the physical and emotional limits we establish to determine who participates and who doesn't participate in specific aspects of our lives. Boundaries are the key to holding these behavioral changes and preventing you from artificially coping or relapsing. With time, the changes in the way you manage your life become solid coping skills. Setting boundaries for yourself, for your behavior, and for others includes the process of learning how to accept those things you cannot control or change.

As researchers, we know there are a few factors that seem to make a long-term difference in recovery. One that regularly stands out in the literature and in our experience is service. When all other ways to cope fail, find a way to serve others—this service will become a coping mechanism. The beginning, middle, and end of coping in recovery should include acts of service. Service gets you outside of yourself, beyond your own problems, and uplifts you and those you serve. Service provides perspective and buffers you so you can overcome the temptations inherent to the process of recovery.

In addition to service, you must change and establish new

rituals and traditions in your life. For many in addiction, family rituals and traditions (e.g., holidays or family reunions) are centered on unhealthy coping behaviors (i.e., drinking, drugging, enabling). Please understand that you may experience a great amount of fear in doing things clean and sober, as this is different from your old way of coping.

How do we learn to engage in these interactions and enjoy them without drugs and alcohol or engaging in other addictive behaviors? First, you must be consistent in doing things differently. You can go to a party where drugs and alcohol are not offered and still enjoy yourself. You can have a conversation with someone without being high. You can be intimate with your partner without using mind-altering drugs. Second, you must exercise patience, given that it takes time to alter your sense of enjoyment. Creating these new rituals, traditions, and behaviors is important as you continue to move away from the pain of the past and cope differently in your life.

Considerations of Healthy Coping Skills

This section is designed to help you think through and apply the concepts addressed in this chapter. As you contemplate and consider developing new ways to cope, keep in mind that developing new ways to manage the pain and stress in your life is a process with both immediate and long-term outcomes. As always, addicts and family members should work through each question as it relates specifically to them.

In this chapter, we taught that a connection to your Higher Power is essential in your pursuit of better ways to cope.

Think about your connection to your Higher Power.

- How connected do you feel?
- How important is this connection for you right now?
- How does being connected to the God of your understanding help in learning new ways to cope?
- What can you do to improve your connection to your Higher Power?
- How important is this connection to your long-term recovery?

We believe it is important for you to develop a team of people around you to support your recovery and to model healthy ways of coping.

- Identify and then make a list of key persons in your life who are supportive to your recovery.
- What strengths do they bring to the table?
- How can they assist you in your journey?
- Create a way to reach these key persons (list of phone numbers, e-mails, and so on). We call this "Recovery 911"; it allows you to reach your team quickly in case of recovery emergencies.

There is an interdependent relationship between your choices and the development of healthy coping skills. Given your old ways of coping (using, anger, lying, enabling, manipulation, guilt, and so on), consider the impact of making more healthy choices.

- Create a list of healthy ways to cope that you believe will work for you or that have worked for you in the past.
- Discuss and seek advice on these new ways to cope with a sponsor, mentor, therapist, or trusted person on your team.

One powerful way to cope is to have someone you trust help hold you accountable for your new ways of coping.

- What person (or persons) in your life would be helpful in holding you accountable?
- Talk to this person (or persons) and ask him or her to be a support to you in this way.
- Have you selected a sponsor as part of your recovery?

Drawing healthy boundaries is part of healthy coping. Think about healthy boundaries (who and what you allow to get close to you and in what way) and how your boundaries need adjusting to help you cope more effectively.

Not allowing your mistakes to disqualify you from recovery is essential to managing your life differently. As Sterling's father advises, you must "stay in the game" and continue to move forward.

- How can you remain in the game even after you have made mistakes?
- How will the process of making amends help you move forward and forgive yourself and others?

- What is the difference between shame and healthy sorrow for past mistakes?

Most addicts and family members not in recovery run extremely hot in their metaphorical temperature. Changing this temperature helps you make better choices and surround yourself with other recovering individuals.

- What is your metaphorical temperature now that you are in recovery?
- Are you starting to "cool" off or are you still running "hot"?
- What changes do you need to make?
- How do you think others will respond to your new recovery temperature?

List the key persons in your life.

- Of those key persons, which ones are running a good recovery temperature?
- Do you need to make changes in your key-persons support system?

As we make changes, family and friends resist change and may, consciously or unconsciously, push you to remain the same.

- What are the non-change forces pushing on you and telling you not to change?
- Who are the people delivering these messages?

- Are you experiencing stress as a result of these messages?
- How are you coping with this stress?
- How could learning to draw healthy boundaries help you with change and the stress that results?

In this chapter, we presented a list of ideas for managing your stress more effectively. These ideas were broken down into three key areas: managing yourself, managing your reaction to stress, and managing the amount of stress.

- Which of the items listed in the chapter make the most sense for you?
- What difference would it make in your recovery if you implemented these items on a consistent basis?

Service is one of the most powerful ways to cope with the difficulties of life. Remember, when all other ways to cope fail, find someone to serve.

- Consider the importance of service in your recovery.
- Consider how regular acts of service could change your life.
- Make a list of people/places you could provide regular and meaningful service to.
- Schedule and then follow through with this service.
- Always take some time to process the feelings experienced in your service efforts.

Family rituals and traditions, often centered on using or unhealthy behavior, are difficult to change. Those persons in good recovery make consistent efforts to create new and more healthy traditions and rituals.

- Think about past rituals and traditions in your family. How do they need to change to support recovery?
- How will you maintain your persistence and patience in creating change in this area of your life?
- Consider establishing new rituals and traditions that are important to you personally.

• • •

Following is a list of coping statements provided to assist you in the ongoing evaluation of your recovery. As you assess yourself based on these statements, remember that recovery is a day-to-day journey that requires some degree of consideration regarding where you have been, where you're at currently, and where you are going. Also keep in mind that developing new and healthy ways to cope is both a process and an outcome. As you move along and progress in your healthy coping journey, you should receive good outcomes/ benefits from coping well.

On the scale provided, assess your level of coping
based on the following statements:

1	2	3	4	5
Very Low Coping	Low Coping	Middle Coping	High Coping	Very High Coping

I can deal with the problems that
arise in my life. _____

I am attaining the skills to better
function in my life. _____

I am managing the problems in my life
in new and healthy ways. _____

I am becoming competent in my
day-to-day functioning. _____

I can handle problems better because
of the skills I have attained. _____

My capacity to cope with life has
increased. _____

▶ If your response pattern falls in the middle to high coping end
of the continuum, then you are on the right track for today.

▶ If you find yourself falling into the middle to low end of the
scale, either you are early in recovery and still learning, or you
are struggling and need to reach out for help.

Achievement
and Accomplishment

MOVEMENT BEYOND THE LIMITATIONS OF ADDICTION
TOWARD PERSONAL ACHIEVEMENT

Achievements and accomplishments are natural results of coping in more healthy ways. Achieving at a level befitting your ability nurtures a sense of pride and restores self-respect. There is a sense of joy, peace, and gratitude that comes when you find a purpose and accomplish something meaningful. Addiction has a way of removing meaning from our lives by directing us away from productive activities to more meaningless pursuits. As you establish a history of meaningful accomplishments, it becomes harder and harder to convince yourself that you have no value. The mounting evidence in your recovery speaks to the contrary—you are a person of worth! You are a "good person capable of great things."

Coping successfully over time nurtures greater achievement and accomplishment. In short, the order occurs as follows: Consistent and good choices lead to the development of better coping skills, which then leads to greater achievements and accomplishments, and ultimately greater self-worth. This journey is illustrated by the following story from Sterling's life.

🖋 After several years in recovery, I returned to school to work on my undergraduate degree on a full-time basis. Leaving a financial planning career and selling many of my material possessions, I moved my wife and three children to a different city. Following the first day of classes, I remember walking home from campus and being almost crippled with anxiety. As a matter of fact, I had to sit down under a shade tree and focus on my breathing just to contain myself. The constant thought in my head was, "What have you done?" I realized I had traded a career for an educational pursuit that I really wanted but never felt capable of accomplishing. My thoughts continued, "You're not supposed to be a student; you're just not one of those smart people."

Through my childhood I remember people telling me I was talented, but I never remember being referred to as bright or smart. Because I never excelled academically in high school, I always questioned how smart I was. I couldn't really disagree, given previous scholastic evidence of a 0.76 GPA (about a D-minus average) in my second semester as a college freshman several years prior. I wondered if maybe I wasn't very smart. The message delivered in my addiction was that I was stupid and not capable.

Given past methods of coping (especially in academic matters), in an effort to calm my anxiety, I would have found a way to get out of this commitment and quit. This was the blueprint of my life prior to recovery: quit, quit, and more quit. Instead, amazingly, I collected myself, went home to my wife, and talked about my feelings. I think I even told her I felt stupid around the smart people at the university.

In terms of my academic career, this was the start of a new way of coping—talking about my feelings and anxieties with the "key person" in my life. After visiting with her, communing with my Higher Power, and reminding myself of how important this educational goal was to me personally, rather than quit, I agreed to go back for one more day. The next day, I began to think, "If I buckle down, rather than run, I can get through another day." This became my new pattern. With each additional day I made it through, I realized I could cope by finishing the task rather than running from it.

The key to this novel approach was the concept of finishing: getting through the day, not the entire four years of college all at once. This became my new goal. Just get through the day. It was my first glimpse or understanding of a one-day-at-a-time perspective and the outcomes possible through its daily application. One day becomes a week, a week becomes a month, a month becomes a year, and before you know it you have an extended pattern of success—you can even see the finish line.

My choice to stay in school and go back to class ultimately led to a different way of coping. My new way of coping, after 1,095 days, led to a college degree and the honor of graduating with a 3.7 GPA. After coping in this manner for an additional 2,190 days, I received a master's degree and a Ph.D. from Texas Tech University.

The miracle for me, a boy who was not supposed to be very smart—certainly not an academic—was that I could now see that my previous negative identity was "perhaps" a lie. There was still a part of me (the "perhaps" a lie part of me) that couldn't accept my success in this arena. It wasn't until a phone call came from the university wanting to recognize my achievements and accomplishments as a student that I considered removing the "perhaps" portion from my newly forming identity.

During this phone call, I was informed that as the top graduate student for the upcoming class it should be my privilege to carry the graduate school banner for commencement. Following this invitation, I heard myself tell the person that I was not interested in carrying the flag and abruptly hung up the phone.

Later, while visiting with my mentoring professor, I mentioned I had received this call. After telling him I had declined the opportunity, he immediately picked up the phone and told the graduate school that I would be carrying the flag. Following his phone call and a look from him that seemed to say, "Are you nuts? What's wrong with you?" he explained to me the honor and accomplishment associated with carrying the banner. He went on to say that it was the honor afforded the top graduate student for the whole university. I was the top student? This just couldn't be! But it was; it could be: I was the top student! It was only then that I really considered that what I had achieved was "perhaps" amazing. I might even be kind of smart.

Thankfully, the "perhaps" portion of my self-dialogue began to fade away, and it became clear to me that I was capable of accomplishing anything I set my mind to. I might even belong in a setting I had previously excluded myself from. This was a major shift in my mind-set and in the way I felt about myself. Despite the positive revelation of this experience, it is important to point out that even after twenty years in an educational environment, feeling like I belong is something I occasionally struggle with and continue to work on to this day. Am I capable? Am I smart? Or am I just an imposter? Usually the best I can muster is that "I'm a good person capable of great things." ✄

As each of you in recovery understands, there are occasions when this "perhaps" mentality returns to your way of thinking. This may be preceded by anxiety or other significant stressors in your lives. These stressors nurture old identities and previous self-doubts. Coping is the key to overcoming this old cycle of behavior that artificially perpetuates the lie—a lie that tells us we are not capable.

Sterling's story punctuates the need for us to make different choices. These choices become more effective ways to cope and eventually lead to more amazing achievements. These achievements further sustain healthy choices and better ways to cope. This is a recovery perspective, one that tells the true story about you, not the lie perpetuated by addiction, stress, and anxiety. This process and the outcomes that result are illustrated as part of the following diagram.

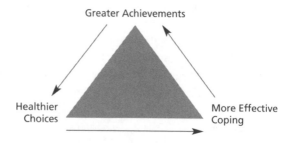

Choices, Coping, and Achievement

Although we will talk about identity in a later chapter, the above diagram should be expanded to include this important concept. The intervening variable between more effective coping and greater achievements is how we think and feel about ourselves—our identity. Identity is shifted, not only by our choices/behaviors and the successes that follow, but also by a nurturing process of cognitive and emotional change that includes positive self-talk and personal affirmation. For example, to this day Sterling combats his "perhaps" self-evaluations with a personal affirmation: he says over and over again while engaging in his exercise routine, "I am a good person capable of great things." Along with other positive self-talk, these efforts help him to overcome the anxiety of the moment and pursue his long-term goals, one day at a time. This process of internal nurturing changes our core beliefs, impacts our ability to make right choices, and benefits from the coping and achievements that follow. Similar core-belief shifts are necessary if you wish to maintain this more effective pattern over the long haul.

Your relationship with your Higher Power is essential to a core-belief shift. Early in recovery your Higher Power offers you a life preserver of sorts. This life preserver represents your Higher Power's more accurate, kind, and loving perspective of who you are and what you are capable of. As with the lifeguard who throws the life preserver, all that is required of you, the drowning victim, is that you reach out and grasp ahold of the offering. In this offering of grace, an exchange between you and your Higher Power occurs. Your God reveals the truth about you, unimpeded by the personal criticism and failures of your past. Through this process, your gifts are uncovered and your potential revealed. This is only the beginning, providing the initial momentum for the day-to-day work required ahead.

As you become more comfortable in your relationship with your Higher Power, day-to-day tasks begin to evolve into the pursuit of your life purposes. In the early stages of recovery, you will find yourself in survival mode. Survival mode is accomplishing the moment-by-moment, day-to-day essentials of life without using. Just making it through the day can be an important achievement. Getting to work on time, paying your bills, and managing the triggers of addiction may seem basic, but they are extremely important to building a foundation of recovery. Being able to take care of your own stuff— "keeping your side of the street clean"—helps you feel better about yourself and begins to change your identity.

After establishing this foundation, the dialectic between you and your Higher Power will eventually produce "higher order," or more meaningful, accomplishments—in essence, your life purposes. Your Higher Power will help you define and highlight the right kinds of accomplishments, to punctuate what is right and good, compelling you toward the right kinds of achievements. As you continue to move forward, your goals will be based in a sense of purpose, a greater vision, and will include more lofty objectives. The basic survival accomplishments, centered on staying clean, evolve into pursuits that allow you to thrive in recovery. For example, thriving pursuits may include gaining a college degree, getting married, obtaining family and relationship success, finding a profession, and attaining financial security.

In the early phases of recovery, you turn your will over to your Higher Power and are coached from above and by those you trust (sponsors, counselors, home groups, the key persons in your life, and so on). The first time you rode a bike, someone was holding you up, pushing you along, and helping you to find your balance. Your journey was guided by those external to you (such as parent, brother, sister, or friend) until you became more steady and competent in your riding skills. Just as with learning to ride, the longer you practice good recovery behaviors and follow the healthy example of others, the more you become capable and better able to determine your own path and unique destiny. It is important to note that this destiny is nurtured by three key factors: (1) the pursuit of God's will in your life, (2) the mentoring of others, and (3) your own life experiences through trial and error.

This process of moving from a place of inexperience and fear (such as riding a bike for the first time) to a place of learning, doing, and accomplishing can be illustrated in an analogy we refer to as the "lone cyclist."

In the early stages of writing this book, we were sitting at a local park talking about ideas and noticed a cyclist pedaling his way up a long hill. He appeared to be motivated and focused on getting to the top. Judging by his effort and progress, he seemed determined to reach his goal despite the myriad of speeding automobiles racing closely past him. In addition to these challenges, he was also riding against a strong West Texas headwind. It was the contrast between the cyclist and the cars around him that most caught our attention. He was undeterred by those who were moving faster and more easily up the hill. When at last he reached the pinnacle, we couldn't help but think how his journey mirrors the journey of those in recovery.

Like the cyclist, the addict has a long and difficult journey ahead. Life is hard, and there are many distractions. Focus is essential if you are to reach your goal. Others will try to convince you that their way up the hill is better or that you should trade in your bike for something faster. Wouldn't it be easier to push the gas pedal to the floor and let the automobile do the work? Or is there something in the one-pedal-after-another focus of the cyclist that is beneficial to you and your recovery?

As with the cyclist, you may feel that you have the whole world buzzing past you in life's journey. You will be tempted to compare your "bike" with what you consider the "luxury vehicles" of those around you. Try to be content with your own gifts and talents and avoid unfair and distracting comparisons.

These types of comparisons will destroy your peace and serenity. Like the cyclist, you need to be confident in who you are and what you are trying to accomplish. Make sure these accomplishments allow you to stretch yourself, yet are reasonable and can be attained. This consideration of attainability can be aided by being realistic about your abilities and drawing upon the gifts given to you by your Higher Power.

As we observed this cyclist, it became obvious to us—due to his physical conditioning—that this wasn't the first hill he had attempted to conquer. He had obviously conquered many others in the past. Be patient with yourself. In achieving and accomplishing your dreams, start with small hills and build up to the longer and more difficult ones. You will become stronger and stronger over time and become more capable of taking on the most challenging purpose-driven goals. As the cyclist did, if you stay on the path you have chosen, you will remain motivated, undeterred, and content with the joy that will result upon reaching the top of the hill. This joy will become the springboard for your next journey and success.

As with the cyclist, staying on the path requires a level of resolve that is illustrated in the healing and recovery portion of Tom's story about his son's cancer:

> In the summer of 2010, we celebrated five years since the end of Nato's treatment. It was a wonderful opportunity for us to remember all we had accomplished and achieved through our experience. It was also a time for us to celebrate the preservation of Nato's life, and more broadly to celebrate life itself.

Today, the emotional roller coaster and difficulties of early treatment seem like a bad memory. Our son, a healthy young man, is far away from his daily struggle with death. At a dinner with extended family to celebrate our life together, I thought to myself, "Wow, we have come so far and learned so much."

The initial strength from our Higher Power combined with the support of family and friends has turned into our own internal strength. This internal strength, forged from the hammer and heat of our adversity, can now be shared with others who struggle.

Through the process, my relationship with my good wife and kids is strengthened. We have gained wisdom and perspective from walking a difficult path together. And, most importantly, we have learned to turn our will and life over to our Higher Power and to trust the journey of each new day. Is our life perfect? No! Is there a chance the cancer will return? Yes! But, we trust that in the end, even with life's imperfections, life will work together for our good. The daily tasks of surviving have evolved into an understanding of the purpose and meaning of life.

Despite the difficult nature of this trial, I can truly say that walking through this experience together has been a blessing. We accomplished something that ranks as one of the most important achievements of our lives. ✒

For those of you who keep a journal of your recovery, we have no doubt that you will write about "internal strength, forged from the hammer and heat of adversity." This internal strength will provide direction for you, wisdom for those around you, and an understanding of the purpose and meaning of your life. As was illustrated with the "lone cyclist," we are certain that you can accomplish the goal of long-term recovery, regardless of the trials and tribulations that will most certainly come.

Considerations of Achievement and Accomplishment

Sometimes the thought of achieving and accomplishing positive, meaningful endeavors brings anxiety. It is important for you to understand that the anxiety surrounding stretching yourself or doing things differently is normal.

- When you feel anxiety about accomplishing your goals, how can you deal with it more productively?

In this chapter, we present the idea that there is a strong connection between coping well and achieving your goals.

- In your addiction or in dealing with an addict, how did you cope with the barriers to reaching your objectives?
- What efforts do you need to make to change these unproductive patterns?
- How would changing old patterns help you achieve your dreams?

In Sterling's story about going back to school, he introduces the concept of having a "perhaps" mentality. Having a "perhaps" mentality means to second-guess or underestimate your accomplishments.

- Are there times when you hold on to your own "perhaps" mentality?
- Remember Sterling's "I'm not smart" message? What negative messages do you carry around about yourself?
- Are there positive messages emerging that you could replace the negative ones with?
- Can you think of yourself as a "good person capable of great things"?

In this chapter, the metaphor of the life preserver is presented. The idea is that if you reach out and grasp the life preserver your Higher Power throws to you, you will be better able to achieve your goals.

- How do you go about grasping the life preserver? How does grasping onto this life preserver help you to achieve and accomplish your life objectives?
- How does remaining connected to this life preserver help you to find more important accomplishments and the purpose and meaning of your life?

Sometimes in early recovery, "accomplishing" means to just take care of the little things in life or just getting through the day. When you are in this "survival mode," you must have patience and not judge yourself on what you hope to achieve as you become stronger in your recovery.

- List your day-to-day tasks that just need to get done and begin doing them.

- Contemplate how doing these mundane things helps to build a foundation of good recovery.
- Can you see how these successes can lead to future victories?

In order for you to begin to accomplish bigger goals—such as education, career, and relationship goals—having a strong connection with your Higher Power is essential.

- List the long-term "higher order" achievements that you would like to see in your life.
- How can your connection with your Higher Power assist you in reaching your aspirations?
- How does knowing that these dreams fit with your Higher Power's will for you help you to move forward, especially when the path becomes difficult?
- Can you trust your High Power even when things aren't working the way you had hoped?

The analogy of the "lone cyclist" is one that compares a cyclist's journey up a long hill to your recovery journey.

- What is it like to consider yourself in the place of the "lone cyclist"?
- Do you ever compare your "bike" to what you consider the "luxury vehicles" of others?
- Contemplate and then list your gifts and talents. If you have trouble coming up with your gifts, ask a trusted sponsor, mentor, therapist, family member, or friend to help you.

- How does practicing good recovery make you stronger for the "long hills," or life's challenges, that lie ahead?

As was the case with Tom and his family when facing childhood cancer, adversity has the potential to build internal strength.

- How can your struggle to overcome addiction and stay in recovery become your strength?
- How can a family who is in recovery together be bound together and achieve and accomplish amazing things?

• • •

The list of statements that follows can assist you in evaluating your level of achievement and accomplishment. As you consider reaching your goals and dreams, remember that the most important achievements take consistent effort, one day at a time. Discovering the purpose and meaning of your life is a continuous process, a lifelong journey. As you consider those things you would like to accomplish in your life and work on them day to day, you should see positive outcomes.

On the scale provided, assess your level of achievement and accomplishment based on the following statements:

1	2	3	4	5
Very Low Achievement	Low Achievement	Middle Achievement	High Achievement	Very High Achievement

I have goals in my life that I want to reach. _____

I am capable of completing things I begin. _____

I am able to recognize my achievement. _____

I have a sense of where I am going in life. _____

I am able to reach the goals I have set. _____

I take care of my responsibilities. _____

▶ If most of your answers fall in the middle to high end of the continuum, you are on the right track for today.

▶ If you find yourself falling into the middle to low end of the scale, either you are early in recovery and still learning, or you are struggling and need to reach out for help.

Capacity for
Meaningful Relationships

THE POSITIVE SUPPORT AND CONNECTION
WITH PEERS AND FAMILIES

Over the years as marriage and family therapists, we have had a front-row seat to amazing stories of relational and recovery successes. We have also witnessed the tragedy of relationships destroyed by untreated addiction or half-hearted recovery efforts. We have great hope for those individuals and families who are able to admit there is a problem and fully embrace recovery. One of the benefits or outcomes of good recovery is a greater capacity to develop and maintain good and healthy relationships. One example of this is shared by Tom below:

🖋 Many years ago I was introduced to a young woman who had just entered into recovery. Her addiction was severe, and when she "hit bottom" it nearly killed her. She was lucky to be alive. As she began her recovery, I remember worrying about whether or not she could really make it. She was so withdrawn and fearful. It was obvious she didn't trust anyone. She struggled to look people in the eye and to accomplish the most basic daily tasks.

Because of her addiction and also because of her past trauma, it was clear that her capacity to be with others early in recovery was very low. She really had no relationships to speak of, since she had no connection with family and had moved to a new place to start over. Despite these obstacles, to her credit, each day she showed up in the places she was supposed to be (recovery meetings, therapy, school). At first, she just sat and observed. She carefully watched and waited. When people approached her to say "Hello" or "Welcome, I'm so glad you came," she would only say a few words in response.

What happened over the next few years is truly the miracle of recovery. Little by little, day by day, I watched this young lady emerge from the pain of her addiction and trauma. The changes were subtle at first. For example, I still remember the first time she looked me in the eye and the first time she disclosed something meaningful about herself. I watched as she began to make friends with others in recovery and even go to coffee or lunch with them. As she continued to move forward, "key persons" emerged, and over time she created a team of supportive people around her. I was grateful to be one of them. Since her family was not in the picture, she literally created a new family made up of those running her same recovery temperature. The outcomes of her recovery efforts included a change in the way she felt about herself, a new level of achievement and accomplishment in her academics and employment, and a close and fulfilling romantic relationship.

Now, several years later and still in recovery, she has a remarkable capacity to be with others. Even more amazing is the number of meaningful relationships she has fostered in her life. She is respected by her friends in recovery, who seek her wisdom and advice for their own recovery. She is also an esteemed helping professional who impacts others in positive ways on a daily basis. Most important, she has found happiness and love with her once boyfriend, now beloved spouse. When she looks me in the eye, I can see the joy that comes with relationship success—relationships that have meaning. 🌿

Addiction impacts our relationships in unique and problematic ways. Along with boundary violations, addiction creates a culture of control, manipulation, and selfishness that strips away the unconditional love/regard and likeability from the relationship. These negative relational dynamics remove the give-and-take in relationships (reciprocity) and further fuel a culture of selfishness. Addiction creates pain for addicts and for those around them. In addiction, emotional and physical boundaries become blurred and are often crossed in our interactions with others. We say and do things that cause pain for ourselves and those around us. The pain created by addiction becomes a barrier that prevents intimacy and meaningful connection.

Moreover, addiction is a disease of secrecy and isolation. For those of you caught in its grasp, it is hard to carry on a relationship with another person when you are hiding something. Your secrets make it impossible for you to look others in the eye, given the shame and blame you carry. It is also hard for others who are observing the addict and the shipwreck that is addiction: they know that the person they once trusted is no longer the captain of his or her own ship—a fact they usually see long before the addict does.

Family and friends are vested in "fixing" the problem, and the addict is vested in continuing to use. Thus, addiction creates competing interests between the addict and those persons who care about the addict. Like a dangerous riptide in the ocean, these competing demands divide and separate the addict from his or her loved ones as the addict is pulled out to sea. Many important relationships won't survive this riptide.

With the pain, anger, secrecy, and conflicts, it is easy to see how addiction removes our capacity for meaningful relationships. Recovery, if done well, can help to restore it. Recovery is the process of learning first how to be with ourselves, and then how to be with others. Hence, one of the most positive outcomes of long-term recovery is your capacity to engage in and maintain meaningful relationships.

Family and relational dynamics have a way of magnifying the problems related to addiction. The way we negotiate relationships is based on systemic guidelines that regulate the nature of our interactions. This regulation occurs through boundaries. Appropriate boundaries are the physical and emotional limits we establish to determine who participates and who doesn't participate in specific aspects of our lives. For example, physical boundaries are the limits you establish that determine whom you allow into your physical space and whom you don't. Emotional boundaries might include the limits you set related to self-disclosure and expressions of emotions. To understand this concept, think about those persons you allow into your emotional space and those you don't. Is there a difference? Why do you let certain people in and keep others out? When these physical and emotional boundaries are not respected or are violated, pain is the result. We also feel pain when we violate the boundaries of others—a pain that we only fully experience when we stop medicating ourselves with drugs and alcohol and begin to feel again.

The presence of addiction increases the probability that boundaries will be violated and pain will be experienced. Recovery is a place where good boundaries are reestablished and should be respected. Violations must not be allowed. The simplest of boundaries is established when we are able to say no to those physical and emotional intrusions that create pain in our lives. Setting important boundaries is one of the keys to finding the health and balance you are seeking. Holding good boundaries—that is, holding the line—is vital to the process of rebuilding trust in your relationships.

In a scene from the movie *Braveheart,* holding the line is illustrated in a powerful way. Scottish freedom fighter William Wallace leads his band of rebels against the British occupiers. In an important battle, the British begin their advance on horseback as the Scottish stand ready. As the British ride down upon them, Wallace yells, instructing his troops to "hold the line!" At the last moment, when the British are almost on top of them, the long-patient Wallace finally exclaims, "Now!"

At that the point, the Scottish raise long, sharpened poles to defend their positions. This was done to stop the advancing cavalry, something that had not previously been accomplished by foot soldiers. As you may remember, the British soldiers and their horses were halted as they were impaled upon the spears. The line was held and the boundary maintained. Over time and in many battles, the Scottish held the line in similar fashion and eventually won their freedom from English bondage.

Freeing yourself from the bondage of addiction requires you to learn how to hold the line. Holding the line on boundaries entails four key elements:

1. **Determine the boundaries that are important to you** without trying to please anyone else. Early in recovery, Sterling cut all ties with his friends in an attempt to preserve his recovery. If you're a family member or friend of an addict, set boundaries that are appropriate for your primary role: parent, sibling, friend, and so on. Don't set boundaries as if you are a therapist, sponsor, or other recovery support person.

2. **Establish boundaries that are well defined, and articulate those boundaries to others.** Remember boundaries are about you holding the line and others learning to respect the line. This also includes you learning how to respect the boundaries of others. As noted above, Sterling set a needed boundary with his friends. Although others thought this was extreme, Sterling held the line because it was important to him and his recovery. His ability to keep this boundary was respectful both to his

friends who were not ready to commit to recovery and to his key persons who needed to observe behavior change in order to reestablish trust.

3. **Protect your boundaries at all costs,** even when the cavalry is riding down upon you. One of the casualties of establishing boundaries was Sterling's relationship with a young woman at the time he found recovery. She couldn't understand why he would set such a boundary and why it had to include her. Several challenges were made regarding his recovery choices and the faith that supported those choices. These came in an effort to "guilt" him into dropping the boundary. Despite the lure, Sterling continued to "hold the line" and resisted falling back into old patterns.

4. **After a period of time, reevaluate the boundaries you have established and make appropriate adjustments.** With time, boundaries that have been consistently held might be able to become more flexible. After several years in recovery, Sterling attended a birthday party thrown for an old friend by his family and, a few years later, a wedding reception for another friend. He felt that these were times when he could be more flexible after years of holding a firm boundary. For both events, he attended early in the evening with his wife (key person), stayed for only thirty minutes, and then left. Over thirty-two years of recovery, these are the only exceptions he has made following his initial decision to sever these ties.

Relationships, like boundaries, can become distorted if addiction is present. The distortion manifests itself in interactions with others that are either way too rigid or too loosely defined. In addiction, individuals and families tend to move to the extremes of the continuum (either rigid or chaotic). The goal in later recovery is to learn how to interact with others in more flexible ways based on the circumstances. Note that boundaries should never be flexible when you are protecting your recovery or yourself (for example, against trauma or abuse).

Adjusting Your Boundaries

Along with boundaries, sometimes unwanted roles are assigned to you or others that are counterproductive to relationship building. These roles may help in the short term but will not maintain stability over the long term. In fact, unhealthy roles can literally spell the doom of important or needed relationships. Historically, unhealthy roles discussed as part of the addicted family include the victim or user, the enabler, the hero, the scapegoat, the lost child, and the mascot. These roles are summarized here as outlined by Wegscheider-Cruse (1981).

Victim/Chemical Dependent: The person who demands the focus of the family. Everything just happens to this person. It is someone else's fault.

Enabler (often the spouse or parent): The caretaker of the family. He or she is the super-responsible one. This person often intervenes so that others do not have to take responsibility for their own actions.

Hero: The person who is going to give legitimacy to the family. The hero represents someone in the family who is "good" as opposed to all of the "bad" family members. As the functioning of the family gets worse, the hero will try harder to succeed.

Scapegoat: The troublemaker in the family. The scapegoat takes the blame for all of the family's problems. This person often withdraws from the family and looks for belonging somewhere else. He or she gets attention in destructive ways and is often a distraction.

Lost Child: The person who spends much time alone or being busy. The lost child has learned to stay out of the whirlwind of the family. He or she receives little attention, whether positive or negative.

Mascot: The family member who brings comic relief into the family. It is the mascot's job to lessen the tension in the family via the use of humor.

Each of these roles is unhealthy and emerges from a family environment where boundaries are crossed and trust is broken. Although each role fulfills a specific purpose in keeping the family together, these roles generate pain and support problematic or addictive behaviors.

While stuck in confining roles and rigid and chaotic boundaries, you become stifled and trapped. Being stuck in this place will ultimately destroy your capacity to be helpful to yourself and to others. Addiction also leads you into senseless clashes over who should perform what tasks and who is not pulling his or her fair share of responsibility. Instead of focusing on creating healthy roles, your time and energy are spent in senseless debate about roles that don't really matter and that are harmful. When individuals and families embrace recovery, old boundaries and roles must collapse and new, more healthy roles and boundaries are created. While immersed in these unhealthy roles, you lose sight of the more important roles of mother, father, sister, brother, and friend. As noted earlier, these are the roles that have the greatest potential to create change and recovery and are most important when considering boundaries that need to be set. These new recovery roles should be flexible, with each individual in the family or relationship having a choice in the role he or she seeks to pursue.

An illustration may help in understanding these concepts. When thinking from a systems perspective, healthy relationships are described as having equal levels of interaction from each person in the relationship (see circle A). This is a relationship where there is give-and-take and each person has an opportunity to equally contribute.

Circle A: Equal Give-and-Take

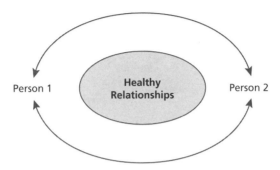

For example, in healthy relationships there is room for each person's ideas. This is represented as a circle where there is an equal level of interaction between each person. This interaction is an open and honest exchange related to feelings, concerns, needs, and wants. There is safety that allows for all parties to interact freely.

In relationships where addiction has been present for long periods of time, there are unequal levels of interaction and each person is not equally contributing. This occurs whether person 2 makes the choice to be there or has been coerced to be there. With either scenario, person 2 is being manipulated by person 1, the addict. The power of the addiction, and the interaction that results, flattens the reciprocal nature of the relationship, and one person dominates over the other (see circle B).

Circle B: Unequal Give-and-Take

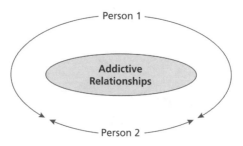

In addiction, one person often dominates the discourse, with no open and honest exchange. This is shown in the diagram by a flat circle that appears to be linear in nature: feelings, concerns, needs, and wants are not openly solicited. One person dominates the interaction. There is no room for personal or relational growth. This flattened discourse is the result of the chokehold of addiction.

The capacity for meaningful relationships is characterized by an understanding that you cannot control another—manipulation is not a healthy option. Manipulation and control are results of addiction and are not characteristics of good recovery. Addiction breeds selfishness. Your consideration of others occurs only when there is something you need or want. In contrast, recovery encourages looking outside of yourself for the mutual benefit of yourself and others. This is a reciprocal relationship, one where each person in the relationship benefits in positive ways.

In their book on families in recovery, Brown and Lewis (1999) discuss the importance of family systems. They propose that old family boundaries, roles, rules, hierarchy, and power structures present in addiction need to collapse, and something new needs to be built in their place in recovery. Like a house, the addicted family's foundation and infrastructure becomes weak and collapses. As individuals and families make the transition to recovery, a new structure, starting from the foundation, must be built. This new structure and those that reside in it must embrace spirituality and the reciprocal relationship with their Higher Power.

The basis of this reciprocal relationship is nurtured within the context of our relationship with our Higher Power. In the first three Steps of the Twelve Steps, we learn how to have a reciprocal relationship with the God of our understanding. For some of you, it may be your first look at a reciprocal relationship. In this sense, "reciprocal" means mutual and shared, or being in a relationship that allows for both give and take. You give up your will to God, and God gives you back the ability to hold on and manage your life and relationships more effectively. This gift or ability expands your capacity to be in relationships where respect and care abound.

In the exchange that occurs between you and your Higher Power, you give up your will to God, who helps you understand a new and better way. Given the selfishness of addiction, this may be the first time you were received unconditionally by another. In these first Steps, you learn how to have a relationship, especially as it relates to your Higher Power. You learn what a meaningful and reciprocal relationship truly is. In contrast to the selfishness and self-centeredness of addiction, you find meaning in your ability to accept the offerings of those around you without attempting to manipulate or control the outcome.

We believe that God only requires the exchange of your will in return for the many gifts provided. However, to maintain a relationship with significant others, family members, and friends, you will be required to give in different ways, beyond that of your will. It is reasonable to consider that those you love will have additional needs and desires. On a broader level, their needs may include love, care, understanding, forgiveness, and consideration. More specifically, they may need attention, praise, kindness, positive interaction, and your time. As you work to become more focused on others, by giving these things, you can expect others to return your efforts by helping you to meet your own needs. This is the cycle of reciprocity.

Maintaining a cycle of reciprocity in your relationships makes all who are involved more likeable. We believe that "likeability" is the key to long-term relationships. Likeability is established by the positive efforts you make in your relationship. For example, when you serve others and they in turn serve you, you like them and yourself better. This service enhances the "likeability factor" within the relationship.

In addition to serving others, your willingness to create a safe place through listening, validating, and giving unconditional regard leads to an increase in your likeability factor.

These efforts increase the probability that you will t same thoughtfulness in return. The practice of these covery skills makes you and the people around you m̲ ̲ ̲ like-able and ensures that your relationships are meaningful and lasting.

It has been our experience, through the years of working in the employee assistance (EA) field and in our private practice with couples and families, that the struggle with addiction efficiently kills relationships by sucking out the give-and-take and subsequently ruining the likeability. In short, the likeability factor drops quickly and significantly. This can be seen in a story as told by Sterling.

🌿 For about two years I worked with a couple where the husband's alcohol use was beginning to take its toll on the relationship. Initially, the couple could see past the drinking behavior to the wonderful potential of their relationship. They had hit it off from the beginning and loved each other dearly. The likeability factor in their relationship was initially high, until his drinking began to cause problems for them and they began to consider the possibility of addiction. Though the wife was pretty certain her husband had a problem, he was absolutely certain that he could stop drinking at any time. But his claim insulated him only for so long before his wife and I called him on his bluff.

His inability to maintain any degree of sobriety over any length of time was the first dagger in the relationship, and it caused his wife to worry that this problem may not go away. She was angry that he couldn't control his drinking and that he regularly lied to cover for his transgressions.

She was even more affected by his inability to own up to his problem and seek help. The only times he would own up was when it appeared that she was going to leave the relationship. Only at these critical times was he able to say (though only for her benefit) that he might have a problem. Once again, he would declare that he would stop drinking, not so much because he thought he had a problem, but because he wanted his wife to stay in the relationship. His inability to be honest with himself and others was the first key factor that damaged his likeability. His likeability quotient was rapidly declining.

Many such declines would follow. As his likeability continued to plummet, the give-and-take in their relationship began to wane. Neither liked the other enough to make the effort. She was mad that he continued to struggle by not admitting he had a problem, and he was angry that she wouldn't let this go and continued to nag him. Both were making demands, but neither was giving what the other wanted.

When they were together doing the things that used to make them happy, the issue of alcohol would come up because she could smell the liquor on him or because he started acting incorrigible. She would ask herself: Is he impaired or not? Is he telling the truth or not? Is he ever going to quit? Am I enabling him by staying?

At this point the major dilemma was that he didn't feel that he had a drinking problem, despite the alcohol continuing to create issues in his life. The second biggest problem was that he was about to lose his wife of many years, despite his declaration that he would do anything to keep her, even quit drinking. But his statement that "I will do anything" never translated into meaningful action. Instead, he isolated himself to hide his use, then became very angry when she didn't want to be with him. He cussed at her and her friends when she tried to find support and have a life outside of their relationship. Often, he become inebriated at parties and other functions and screamed at his wife or anyone else who crossed his path.

Over about eighteen months, his likeability plummeted, as did hers. He became locked in his role as the victim or scapegoat, and she was so busy trying to police him that she couldn't play her most important role of wife and lover. According to him, she was simply a nag who had ruined their whole relationship with her demands. The give-and-take in the relationship stopped and was replaced by selfish agendas. His agenda was as follows: I will take her freedom and force her into this relationship. I will keep her away from friends and family so she doesn't have anything else to do but be with me. I will sabotage her business ventures so she will not have any other way to support herself.

In fairness, she had an agenda as well. In an effort to punish him and get him to change, she had distanced herself from him and began pursuing interests she knew would make him angry. Despite this tactic, she would express fear for her safety, especially if she didn't stay with him—a fear that kept her in the relationship, rather than prompting her to leave.

As could be expected, this couple eventually divorced. After eighteen months of trying, they got nowhere. Likeability dropped like a lead balloon, and the previous give-and-take in the relationship came to a screeching halt. Neither felt they had enough internal resources to continue, despite their desire to be together. ✒

This story illustrates the problems that arise for those who are unable to admit they have a problem and to seek the necessary help. It also represents how, over time, likeability quotients can drop and ultimately kill a relationship. Had the husband in this story been able to sincerely admit his problem and reach out for help, the relationship could have been salvaged. If the wife could have embraced recovery for herself and ceased to enable her husband by staying, the current structure of their relationship might have crumbled, letting the necessary rebuilding begin. Without these important changes, the likeability in the relationship was destroyed. With each decline this couple became less connected and the give-and-take in the relationship ceased to exist.

Addictive behavior will *always* root out the likeability, and ultimately the trust, in relationships. When addiction is present in a relationship, trust is what suffers the most. As in Sterling's story, when someone (whether alcoholic, addict, or family member) can't admit he or she has a problem and continues to engage in destructive behaviors, such actions strike at the heart of trust in the relationship. It's as if the lies and the manipulation are bombs blowing up the bridge between partners. The initial lie—"I don't have a problem" or "I promise I will stop"—breeds other lies when the actions of the person contradict the statements made. Learning to trust is the beginning point of expanding and rebuilding your capacity to be with others. Without this foundation, everything will fall apart. Remember that the presence of addiction, and the unhealthy relationship dynamics that result, have destroyed the original bridge. The bridge must be rebuilt one brick at a time.

The beginning of trust occurs when the addict and the family member turn their will over to their Higher Power and admit there is a problem. The process of humbly turning your power over, and the subsequent admission that you can't "fix" the problem without God's help, breeds trust—especially with those closest to you. If you have another person to walk through the difficulties of early recovery with you, together in this walk you become bound and have greater potential to repair the bridge of trust between you.

According to Gottman and Silver (2004), leading authors on marriage and divorce, relationships need to shift to a more favorable positive-to-negative ratio. If relationships are to survive and the bridge of trust is to be rebuilt, positive interactions must exceed the negative ones. To help create a positive cycle of reciprocity in your important recovery relationships, we recommend using the six principles to "Make Your Relationships a Place Where You Both Want to Be" (outlined in Shumway and Wampler, 2002).

1. **Salutary Recognition (Greetings):** Individually acknowledging each other throughout the day in verbal and nonverbal ways. Verbal greetings can take the form

of a simple "Hello" or a "Hey, how was your day?" Nonverbal greetings such as a hug, kiss, or touch of the hand are just as important, if not more.

2. **Small Talk:** Talking with your spouse about the things he or she wants to talk about, no matter how unimportant you might judge them to be. It's important that we set aside time to engage in this process—if we don't, it will never happen. When small-talking, you should avoid topics that may lead to tension or argument (finances, politics, extended family, and so on).

3. **Ego-Building Comments (Praise):** Praising your spouse for the positive things he or she does and for who he or she is. When your spouse does something thoughtful or nice, it is important to praise him or her for the effort. Examples might include "You did a great job handling the finances this month" or "I sure was proud of the way you handled the kids last night." However, despite the importance of these comments, it is just as important to praise your spouse for who he or she is—these are comments that our spouses don't have to do anything to receive. Examples might include "Wow, you're beautiful," "You're nice to be around," "You sure are a great person," or "I'm so lucky to be married to you."

4. **Exciting Activities:** Regularly engaging in activities that both of you find enjoyable and exciting. These activities don't have to be exotic or expensive; they just require

you to block off some time to be together. Activities might include going to the park, going out for dinner or a movie, putting the kids to bed and watching some television together, or just sitting in your car and talking.

5. **Expanding Shared Memories:** Making an effort to create positive memories within your relationship and then reminiscing about those memories. Looking at old pictures, talking about the crazy things you did when you first met, or just talking about the wonderful time you had last weekend at the lake are all opportunities to build the kind of bond that will last a lifetime.

6. **Feedback:** Mutual honesty between spouses. There are two important parts to effective feedback: (1) encouragement when your spouse does something well, and (2) being able to express your concern when your spouse does something wrong. Each of these must occur within a relationship where there is listening, understanding, and validation.

These six things are critical in the rebuilding of likeability and trust in relationships and recovery. Practicing these behaviors has the potential to create miracles, including healing, understanding, and forgiveness between you and those you love. Ultimately, the practice of these things leads to greater relationship satisfaction, likeability, and an increasing capacity for meaningful relationships.

Considerations of Capacity for
Meaningful Relationships

A key to this chapter is your understanding of boundaries and the importance of establishing and holding healthy boundaries in the process of relationship building. Remember, a boundary can be set as easily as saying no.

- List the people you allow to be close to you in physical ways (including sexual) and in emotional ways.

- Have you experienced pain from people crossing your boundaries or pain when you crossed the boundaries of others?

- Do you continue to experience the guilt, shame, and grief of boundaries that have not been respected, whether by you or by someone else?

- Are there some old boundaries that need to be rebuilt or remodeled?

- What new boundaries do you need to establish in recovery?

- Are you capable of saying no? Is there someone you need to say no to?

The confining roles we play in addiction often cause pain. When we are in these unhealthy roles, we often do and say things that we normally would not.

- What unhealthy roles have you played in your life?

- What unhealthy roles are you playing right now (for example, victim, enabler, hero, scapegoat, lost child, mascot)?

- Are you in these roles by choice or were they assigned to you by family members?

- If you could create your own healthy roles in recovery, what would they be?

- What would it be like to let old boundaries and roles collapse and rebuild new ones on a foundation of recovery?

- Have you considered your most important role lately— that of father, mother, sister, brother, husband, wife, friend, and so on?

- How would your life be different if you began to focus on these roles and stopped functioning in the less healthy roles associated with addiction?

Selfishness, manipulation, and control are hallmarks of unhealthy relationships. These strategies must change if we wish to expand our capacity to be with others.

- In what ways have you been manipulated and controlled?

- In what ways have you manipulated and controlled others?

- How will the process of making amends for using these strategies in the past help you heal and have better relationships in the future?

- Can you begin to forgive others for their boundary violations? Are you seeking amends for your own boundary violations?

- Imagine what it would be like to be in relationships where there is equal give-and-take, where your feelings are honored and you can be honest.

We believe reciprocal relationships start with your relationship with your Higher Power.

- How does your relationship with the God of your understanding help you expand your capacity to be with others? Discuss this with a trusted sponsor, mentor, therapist, friend, or family member.

Alcoholism/addiction kills the "likeability" in relationships. As you continue on in your recovery, your level of likeability should improve (your likeability quotient will increase).

- What is your likeability quotient?
- What does being likeable mean?
- With the ideas presented in this chapter in mind, how would you go about increasing your likeability in your recovery?
- What do you need from others for them to be more likeable to you?

Sterling's story about the couple who couldn't reach out for meaningful help in their relationship, and because of the husband's addiction eventually divorced, is all too typical.

- Who do you relate to in the story and why?
- What needs to change in your relationships for you to

make sure the consequences outlined in the story don't happen to you?

Addiction and the subsequent pain and sorrow destroys the bridge of trust between people. Recovery has the potential to rebuild the bridge, one brick at a time.

- Make a list of those things you can do to rebuild trust with your family and other loved ones. Where appropriate, begin to do those things.
- Consider any amends you need to make.
- How does the process of trust building relate to your capacity to be with others?
- What role does humility play in the process of trust building?
- Who can you trust right now?
- Who do you most need to develop trust with?
- Where can you turn for guidance in this effort?

• • •

Following is a list of statements to assist you in evaluating your capacity for meaningful relationships. Building healthy relationships in recovery takes time and is a day-to-day journey. As you continue to surround yourself with those who support your recovery and are willing to work hard with you, you should see your relationships improve.

On the scale provided, assess your capacity for meaningful relationships based on the following statements:

1	2	3	4	5
Very Low Capacity	Low Capacity	Middle Capacity	High Capacity	Very High Capacity

My relationships are stable. _____

I reach out to others in times of need. _____

I feel connected to others. _____

My ability to have close relationships is improving. _____

Relationships with those I consider family are more healthy. _____

There are others in my life I can depend on for support. _____

▶ If your pattern of answers falls in the middle to very high end of the continuum, then you are on the right track for today.

▶ If you find yourself falling into the middle to low end of the scale, either you are early in recovery and still learning, or you are struggling and need to reach out for help.

Unique Identity Development

THE EMERGENCE OF A UNIQUE AND POSITIVE PERSONAL IDENTITY

At any given point in the process of recovery, how you feel about yourself will provide either the motivation for continued success or the trigger for failure. Considering the power a person's identity has to encourage positive outcomes or nurture defeat, it is important that you assess your own identity as part of the process of recovery. Our professional work and personal experience have taught us that addiction nurtures feelings of worthlessness, guilt, and shame. The message from those around you and from within yourself is that you don't have anything to offer. This couldn't be further from the truth.

In the initial steps of reaching out to your Higher Power, you begin to get impressions and feelings that contradict this negative feedback. Even considering these new messages, it is hard to believe that you have worth and that you have something to offer. It may be the first time that you have felt this type of unconditional love and acceptance that can be given so abundantly by your Higher Power and the key people in your recovery. For the first time, you begin to understand who you really are and who and what you are capable of becoming. As you move forward in your recovery, the negative messages of the past begin to fade, replaced with something new and wonderful: "I am a good person capable of great things!"

Our negative identity and the demeaning self-talk that follows are nurtured from an early age as we become a repository for other people's judgments of our worth. In all of our imperfections, we as human beings are inclined to believe the erroneous things people say about us—we buy them hook, line, and sinker. This is compounded when we hear these things at an early age or over the course of many years. The impact of these negative messages is further magnified when addiction is present during our early development. Though we may argue with others' judgments on the outside, on the inside we absorb them like a sponge. However, unlike a sponge, the water remains unevaporated over a lifetime, weighing us down and maintaining our pain.

While working on his Ph.D., Sterling learned about and experimented with certain methods of changing how a person engages in self-talk. His effort to implement these methods in his own life was a culmination of the study of multiple self-help resources and professional efforts in his private therapy practice.

🌿 After studying multiple cognitive strategies related to the art of changing self-talk, I found one that stood out to me. It involved changing the nature and frequency of such talk. The idea was to encourage people struggling with negative internal messages to write down positive affirmations related to themselves and say them over and over each day, as many times as possible.

This was a tall order, made taller when the theory behind this technique was understood. A person's inner self would literally fight against the positive affirmations, making the person even more troubled before experiencing improvement. In essence, the claim is that the subconscious (as it is sometimes called) was so used to a steady diet of negative self-talk that it would recoil at the change in diet and begin to fight back. Thus, the person's subconscious would reject the positive messages in favor of the negative ones. This rejection would cause pain in the initial stages of the process.

With this information in mind, I decided to develop a list of three positive things about myself and write them on a sheet of paper. I then taped the paper on my wall in the bedroom where I could see it from my treadmill. Each night I would get on my treadmill and rehearse these three things over and over again, until my workout was complete.

For the first week, everything went great. I enjoyed the treadmill and the positive affirmations that seemed to provide motivation to my workout. However, this joy was short-lived. During the second week, I began to abhor the thought of getting on the treadmill. An activity that I had loved only a few days previously became a chore of monumental proportions. By week three, I was miserable. My inner self seemed to be engaged in an all-out war with these positive affirmations; I could barely even get on the treadmill. It got so bad I would dread the thought of having to work out all day long.

Just as the theory goes, my inner self was so used to a steady diet of negatives that it could not process these positive ones. My response was similar to that of a child who ate a whole birthday cake in one sitting: the stomach is so unaccustomed to such a thing that it rejects it, throwing it up. My inner self, or subconscious, was rejecting the positives and attempting to eject them from my system—metaphorically trying to throw them up.

I continued to pursue the task, despite the emotional nausea I was experiencing. To my relief, by the fourth week the struggle began to fade and the benefits of the exercise began to shine through. My workout on the treadmill became a joyful and positive experience. I was able to run faster and was more motivated to keep going for longer periods of time. The endorphins that always accompanied me during this type of exercise were so abundant that I could feel them tingling in the back of my head. It reminded me of the kind of feeling you might have at a really good concert, when experiencing a good sermon, or when seeking the thrills of a good risk-taking endeavor (such as cliff diving, barefoot waterskiing, or car racing). I had stayed in the game and had continued with the effort, despite the pain. I had outlasted the "pain curve" that can discourage us from change and keep us from the prize. 🍃

Change is difficult because of the pain that results. More often than not, the pain prevents us from getting over the hump and experiencing the benefit that awaits us on the other side. If we stay in the game and continue working toward the prize after the time we would normally quit, the benefits will begin to be manifest. Remember the benefits appear at about the same time we would normally give up due to the pain—the pain curve.

Recovery should bring a core identity shift, a shift where you become capable of saying and believing something different than you did in the past. This process of rehearsing the positive messages in your mind and heart is what we refer to as "value-nurturing." In the process of value-nurturing, there is a constant effort to consider your accomplishments and rehearse them over and over in an effort to drive them to a deeper level. This deeper level is where we begin to believe the messages and do things for the right reasons. The value-nurture occurs when you consider the meaning of your accomplishments and then assess your own thoughts and feelings about your achievement.

A good example of value-nurturing is illustrated in Sterling's story about being the top honor graduate.

🖋 On the occasion of my graduation, my wife asked me, "What's it like to be honored as the top graduate student at Texas Tech?" After my first response, which was to joke it aside as luck or some mistake by the university, this question provided me the opportunity to develop my own internal discourse as to why I deserved to be the top graduate and how it made me feel. It really didn't matter what everyone else thought about my accomplishment. What really mattered was whether or not I could see and feel the value my achievement had for me. Had it not translated into an internal belief in myself and caused my identity to shift, it would have been as if it never happened. For me, the shift occurred when I was able to respond to my wife's question in a way that celebrated my accomplishment and nurtured some hope in my own heart that "perhaps" the honor was deserved. 🌿

Tom has seen this value shift occur with his own children when nurturing their academic accomplishments and achievements.

🌿 When my children receive good report cards, I praise them, then I ask, "What's it like to be so smart?" In their young eyes, I can actually see the shift from the external compliment I am giving to their own internal evaluation. At one moment they are looking for external praise and validation from their dad, and in the next moment they are really considering how this accomplishment makes them feel and what it means to them. It's an amazing thing to have them look back at me with a smile and say, "It makes me feel good, Dad, and it's really cool." 🌿

In summary, the key to value-nurturing is when the individual begins to verbalize and internalize the value of his or her accomplishment. When Tom's child says, "It makes me feel good, Dad, and it's really cool," it's clear that his child has developed an internal discourse as to why getting good grades is important to him or her. Over time, this becomes part of the child's core identity as a person. Similarly, with Sterling the value-nurture occurred when he was able to consider that the honor he was given was deserved, as opposed to the old message, rooted in addiction, that he wasn't very smart.

As was the case with Tom's kids, children may have a parent or friend (key person) who can offer the praise and follow it with the value-nurture question. However, some of you may not have or may never have had a supportive key person in your life. The value-nurture process may have to be something you do within yourself. Without supportive others to offer the praising comments and ask the value-nurture question, you will have to ask the questions and consider the answers on your own. To help you with this, the value-nurturing process is further described below.

> **Value-Nurturing:** Learning to do important things for the right reasons. In other words, once a positive action is occurring consistently, you then work on getting that action to occur for the right reason—because you feel good about doing it and it fits with your recovery perspective. Feeling good about your actions and yourself is the goal of value-nurturing.

A possible sequence for value-nurturing is outlined below.

1. When something has been achieved, consider the benefit of what you just accomplished or what the person you are value-nurturing has accomplished.

2. See the positive in what they or you have accomplished.

3. If you are value-nurturing for someone else, praise that person. If you are value-nurturing for yourself, praise yourself by considering the positive things you have done.

4. Continue the positive praise when accomplishments are reached. Begin to ask the value-nurture question of yourself or of the person you are value-nurturing: "How does it make you feel inside when you do that?" or "How does it make you feel when you are so successful?"

The value-nurture question allows you or the person you are nurturing to begin to formulate personal reasons for engaging in a particular task or behavior. Over time, this nurtures new and long-lasting behaviors and changes identity from the inside out. Remember, this is a process that needs to be engaged in over the long haul.

As you value-nurture, new and more accurate beliefs about yourself should be heard and internalized, given consideration, and reinforced by the achievements and accomplishments of your life (see the diagram here).

**Coping Differently
through Value-Nurturing**

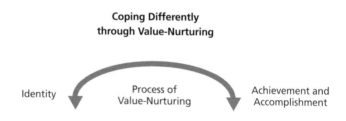

Identity → Process of Value-Nurturing → Achievement and Accomplishment

Early in the process, you establish a general identity, such as "I am a good person!" As you move forward in the hope of recovery, you begin to cope differently and develop a track record of accomplishments. You begin to understand your unique gifts and talents, and you develop a very specific and unique identity. With this specific identity, you will begin to find a place of self-acceptance where you believe that you are "a good person capable of great things."

As noted in chapter 3, identity is an important variable when considering choice, coping, and achievements. A simple way to understand the progression of identity in recovery is illustrated in the next diagram. As you make healthy choices over time, it leads to a pattern of coping more effectively. Coping more effectively leads to a greater level of achievement and accomplishment. These achievements begin to provide support for a more positive identity. In general, the progression

Building a Positive Identity

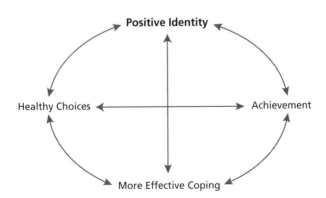

usually starts with making good choices, which then leads to better coping, to greater levels of accomplishment, and to a more positive identity. But at some point in your recovery each of these starts to impact the other in a more circular fashion. This dynamic is represented by the arrow lines in this diagram, representing the interchange between each of these attributes. As with the Twelve Steps, you never fully graduate from any one attribute. Instead, you are constantly monitoring all of them and how they impact each other.

We have discussed the need to change our negative identities to more positive ones in recovery. The process of developing a new identity has some pitfalls that should be considered. Some of these pitfalls include others trying to determine your identity through contradictory messages. They heap their expectations upon you and attempt to hijack your identity. Other stumbling blocks may include your use of old and outdated perceptions of yourself—the negative ones that were nurtured in your addiction. These negative perceptions of yourself don't allow you to reach new and important goals; hence, they reinforce the idea that you are worthless and unable to achieve and accomplish. Feelings of worthlessness produce pain, and pain precedes relapse.

Early on in the process of addiction, everyone else seems to have an idea of who you are and what you should become. Often the messages you heard as a child were contradictory. On one hand, people told you that you were a "problem child" and "not very smart," but that you had all the potential in the world, if you would just change your ways. Sound familiar?

The external message is that "you could be so amazing" or "you have so much potential if you could just stop using." All you heard was the "not very smart" portion of the message. It's as if someone gives you a compliment such as "You did a great job . . . *but* you can always do better." All the addict can hear is what comes after the "but"—"you can do better." The "great job" portion of the message gets lost in the negative that follows.

In addition to the contradictory message, there are unrealistic expectations embedded in the messages of others. The message is that you must meet all of your unrealized potential and become an amazing person. These are external messages that may not be congruent with your plan for yourself. The expectations of others for you to conquer the world may require goods that you're not yet convinced you possess. The difference between others' expectations and the expectations you have for yourself may create dissonance, anxiety, and feelings of depression. If you believe you will fail and never live up to the expectations of others, it may seem easier to just be the scapegoat, stoner, or failure that others have suggested you might be. In this place of unrealized expectations, it would seem easier to turn the plane over to the hijackers and have your destination determined for you. The problem is the dissonance that follows when you realize you haven't been honest with others, and more importantly, with yourself. You will never find lasting joy if you allow others to hijack your identity.

Addicts, enablers, and other family members often filter

their achievements through a lens that emphasizes what they *haven't* accomplished versus what they *have.* It is easy to retreat to the extremes of the continuum where you don't do anything because you haven't accomplished *everything*—and this is like throwing the baby out with the bathwater. In an effort to find value in yourself, you throw out all of the good because somehow you haven't been perfect. It's a constant battle to cut yourself some slack, to allow for the addiction in your life, and to find value in the person you are. In early recovery it is OK to be good; you don't have to be perfect or great. It's not necessary to know, be, and do everything. Good recovery allows you to be who you are, embracing the gifts and talents you already possess. Good recovery also helps you to understand who you can become and the one-day-at-time perspective it takes to get there.

The way in which you overcome the pitfalls of expectation and perfection requires the development of good boundaries and the ability to block unhelpful messages and unrealistic expectations. You must also learn to say no to such messages and to the people who are delivering them. Saying no is an internal and external pursuit. Internally, you are rejecting the negative message and replacing it with your own realistic and appropriate message. Externally, you need to say no to those persons who continue to hijack your identity and heap unrealistic expectations on you. In short, you let them know you don't appreciate their feedback. In extreme cases, you may need to cut them out of your life completely. The emergence of your own positive, unique identity is worth the anxiety and discomfort of holding important boundaries.

As you draw these boundaries and take this proactive stance, you will occasionally hear messages from the past. These messages from the past may include negative and self-defeating comments such as "You can't do that," "You'll never finish anything," or "You're just an imposter." Don't listen to this negative self-talk. Just keep moving forward. With some occasional intrusion (particularly early in recovery), these negative messages will eventually fade.

Often this negative self-talk comes at a place of early recovery or potential relapse. In one critical moment, the demons of addiction swoop in and attempt to steal your identity and return it to an outdated, less positive one. It would be easy for you to accept this invitation and think that you have returned to square one. This is a lie. You may have relapsed and have to change your "dry date," but you have not thrown away all the progress you attained in the pursuit of recovery. When considering issues of identity, your recovery date should reflect the number of years you have been in recovery. Changing your dry date should not wipe away all the learning and experience gained in your recovery.

You may need to reach out for help from your Higher Power or another who can reinforce your positive efforts. When all else seems to fail, serve someone less fortunate than yourself. Serving helps you see your own value and put your own journey into perspective. Let your Higher Power and your positive actions confirm to you that you are a "good person capable of great things."

If you relapse, quickly return to your efforts at maintaining your recovery. You do this by reaching out for help and nurturing the positive messages of recovery. By reaching out quickly, you may avoid the pain of a total regression—which will happen if you continue to use—and be able to pick up recovery where you left off.

An additional factor to consider is the shift in identity you receive upon entering recovery. When you enter recovery, you are asked to admit you're an alcoholic/addict and declare your desire to find recovery. Particularly early in recovery, this is an important identity, as it attaches you to others who have experienced addiction and are seeking recovery. This connection is helpful in gaining an understanding of yourself and the context in which you practiced your addiction. The benefit of this connection and the understanding that follows is that when other people share their stories, you are better able to validate without judgment. Learning to have empathy for others allows you to more fairly judge them based on the context of their lives. As a result, you learn to have empathy for yourself and see the entire picture of your addiction. This empathy for others and the subsequent empathy that develops for yourself is one of the great outcomes of good recovery.

While you move forward in your recovery, your identity will grow to encompass other more broad categories of life. You will see yourself as more than just an addict in recovery and will achieve and accomplish other things. You will see your value in other more important roles as mother, father, husband, wife, or friend. As you excel in these other roles of life, your identity will become positively complex. A good visual is a tree that grows and branches off in many directions. As the tree grows, it becomes more expansive and is more capable of surviving. Similar to the tree, the trunk, or foundation, of your recovery will support your growth in all areas of your life. As Sterling reports:

> At this stage in my life, I identify myself as a good husband, a good father, and a good friend. I am also a tenured professor and therapist. I am a leader in my church community, and my service to others seems to make a difference. I consider myself a good neighbor and contribute to my community. All of these roles identify the tree that has emerged from my life of sobriety. Oh, and by the way, I am also in recovery.

Considerations of Unique Identity Development

The emergence of a positive identity is the outcome of the journey you are making in recovery. The types of messages you believe about yourself are clues to the current state of your identity—positive or negative.

- What are the positive messages you carry about yourself?
- What are the negative messages you carry about yourself?
- Where do these negative messages come from?
- How would discussing these messages with your Higher Power and other key persons help in your recovery journey?

We believe that value-nurturing may help you change your identity to a more positive one.

- After doing something well, or after someone else offers you praise for a job well done, add this question: "How does doing _____ make me feel about myself?"

- Make a commitment to value-nurture yourself each morning and night and throughout the day by reviewing how you feel about your positive accomplishments. Remember to regularly consider that you are a "good person capable of great things."

- If you are an addict's family member, make a commitment to value-nurture yourself. Consider how you can offer value-nuturing to the addict in your life as well.

Refer back in the chapter and consider how value-nurturing might assist you in changing your identity or someone else's.

- How might the process of value-nurturing help you stay in recovery?

Consider Sterling's story about affirmations he repeated while walking on his treadmill.

- What positive affirmations do you need to say over and over to assist in your identity growth?

- What difference would it make in your life if you continually said to yourself, "I am a good person capable of great things"?

We believe there is a strong connection between healthy choices, effective coping, achievements, and a more positive identity.

- How do you experience the connection between these recovery attributes?
- Are you beginning to make healthier choices and cope more effectively?
- How is your identity benefiting from these effects?

Evaluate your progression from healthy choices to greater levels of coping, to achievement and accomplishments, and to a more positive identity.

- How will a more regular consideration of these things impact your recovery in a positive way?
- How will they impact your identity—or have they done so already?

In this chapter, we identified a number of pitfalls to your emerging positive identity.

- What are the contradictory messages you have received in the past about yourself?
- List the unrealistic expectations that others have set for you.
- Which of these expectations have you believed "hook, line, and sinker"?
- When you embrace the unrealistic expectations, whose lens are you viewing them through?

- When considering the expectations above, identify the ones that are clearly inaccurate.
- How does learning to have and hold good boundaries help you to move past the negative messages and unrealistic expectations?

Relapse is an important area to discuss. Ideally, you will enter into recovery and remain in recovery without relapse as part of the equation. Unfortunately, people do relapse. Remember that your recovery should reflect all the time you've spent recovering, not just the time since your dry date.

- How can confronting the lies and whispers of old identities help you stay away from relapse?

If you find yourself in a state of relapse, reach out for help as quickly as possible. In relapse, it is important to remind yourself that you can be in recovery once again.

- How does changing your dry date differ from counting all your time in recovery?

We believe that recovery represents the trunk of your life's tree and that the branches are other parts of your identity that you will nurture.

- Identify the branches of your identity tree that are already thriving.
- What other branches of your identity do you need to add to your trunk?

• • •

Following is a list of statements to assist you in evaluating the emergence of your recovery identity. As you consider your identity within the context of these statements, keep in mind that recovery is a day-to-day journey. Creating a new positive identity is an ongoing process. As you think about and work the strategies outlined in this chapter and your connection with your Higher Power, you should see the benefits and outcomes of having a more positive identity.

On the scale provided, assess your identity
based on the following statements:

1	2	3	4	5
Very Negative Identity	Negative Identity	Neutral Identity	Positive Identity	Very Positive Identity

I am developing into the person I want
to be.   _____

I am learning to accept myself for who I am.   _____

I like the person I am becoming.   _____

I know who I am.   _____

I am making progress as a person.   _____

I recognize my growth and development
as a person.   _____

▶ If your pattern of answers falls into the neutral to positive
   identity category, then you are on the right track for today.

▶ If you find yourself falling into the neutral to negative end
   of the scale, either you are early in recovery and still learning
   about yourself, or you are struggling and need to reach out
   for help in your recovery.

Reclamation
of Agency

THE INTERNAL FEELING THAT YOU HAVE CHOICES IN YOUR BEHAVIOR—INCLUDING THE CHOICE NOT TO USE

Reclaiming one's agency is the ability to make appropriate choices, a skill previously lost in your addiction. True agency is realized when you are able to make choices in your life, unfettered by compulsion, addiction, or the manipulation of others. The choices that you make should be decided on within the context of your renewed relationship with your Higher Power. When decisions are made within this context, your agency/choice becomes purposeful, focused, and proactive. This is in complete contrast to the choices made while actively involved in your addiction. Past life choices were often random, impulsive, chaotic, and reactive. In relation to your addiction, there was *no* choice. You were going to use regardless. This is the nature of addiction. When agency is reclaimed, you are not acted upon by the addiction or some outside influence, but are acting as an agent unto yourself, under the direction of your Higher Power.

When addiction is present, your relationships suffer and are supplanted by the substances of your addiction. Even your Higher Power is squeezed out of your life as your power to choose is crowded out by your addiction. You become dependent on drugs or alcohol and forget to depend on your Higher Power and the other key persons in your life. You slowly move down the continuum of addiction where your choices are determined for you. These choices are made not with the assistance of the God of your understanding, but by your drug of choice. You have lost your agency, your ability to choose your own life. Refer to the continuum shown in the diagram here.

The Journey to Addiction

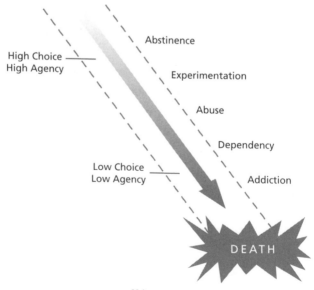

Before you experienced addiction/alcoholism, and the obsession and compulsion that comes with it, you probably remember being able to make the choice not to use. You could look at a beer or watch others get high and not be tempted to partake. For those of you who found it quite natural to be an addict, you might have to go back to a very early time in your life to find this place. As you progressed in your addiction, from experimentation to abuse to dependence—as shown in the diagram—you slowly but surely lost your ability to make good choices, the most important of which was not to use.

At the point of addiction, the question of "if" you will use is already answered—you will! The only questions that remain are "When?" and "How often?" Using is no longer a choice you make, but a behavior you will engage in regardless of your intent or desire. Given that you are going to use, your only real choice would be to raise your hand and ask for help. Reaching for help is not usually a priority in addiction; all too often an addict does so only after "hitting bottom."

Addiction/alcoholism is like an eclipse. During a solar eclipse, the sun's rays are blocked by the moon. The sky darkens as the rays of the sun become impeded and are not able to shine directly on the earth. In this eclipse metaphor, addiction plays the role of the moon and begins to block the warming rays of hope offered by your Higher Power. When addiction is running rampant and the eclipse of addiction is in full gear, the transactions between you and your Higher Power become less abundant and less clear, and have less impact. It is hard to see or benefit from the sunlight of the spirit through the darkness of addiction. Recovery begins when you realize your predicament and turn "your will and your life" over to God. As you learn to manage the eclipse of addiction and maintain your connection with God, you begin to slowly reclaim your agency and make better and healthier choices. Eventually, you regain some semblance of choice and are able to determine your own destiny in relationship with your Higher Power.

Addiction produces a life that is predetermined—it is a forced path of pain, sorrow, and remorse. Recovery allows for broader purposes to appear, for your Higher Power to have a say in your life, and for you to have the final veto power in your destiny. It is a path where you literally purchase back a day's worth of choice for each day you stay in recovery. With this choice comes a freedom from compulsion and addiction and the ability to release the shackles that have bound you, determining your daily endeavors and the misery that followed.

Early in recovery, choices are made on a moment-by-moment, day-to-day basis. Sometimes just getting through the day is the goal. However, in the later stages of recovery, choices can be made that reach beyond the day-to-day and allow you to see and plan for the future. Through these recovery efforts (process) you are able to behold a glimpse of your future (outcome). Different from the narrow view of early recovery, this broader look provides an image of attainable objectives. This broader vision becomes the motivation for your daily walk, as opposed to simply making it through the day. You move to a place where you can achieve and accomplish something bigger and better. Here the real motivation of recovery kicks in and begins to offer up more compelling reasons for living in an environment that doesn't include drugs and alcohol.

As you move forward and the "beer goggles" (clouded vision) begin to fade, you are able to see the long-term impact of your choices. Be patient! Initially you will not be able to see the entire map of your life, but only the emerging trail in front of you, which will provide for your daily walk. Keep following the trail, and eventually the whole map will unfold to your understanding. For those who have yet to experience this rebirth, we want you to know that it is well worth your day-to-day struggle to achieve. It will change your whole outlook on life and provide you with a different set of goggles, a set prepared for you and provided via the ongoing relationships between you, your Higher Power, and the other key persons in your life.

Don't forget that this process takes time—all of the other five principles discussed in this book need to be understood, considered, and integrated as part of your recovery. They provide important resources to support and sustain your recovery walk and to better insure against relapse and regression. Though you will regress at times, you want to make sure that with each step you take forward you don't also take a step backward. You must have a net gain of steps in your recovery or you will never reach beyond your current state and become all that you can be.

As you progress in your recovery and make healthy choices, you begin to pay back the spiritual loan you received from your Higher Power. Though you flirted with bankruptcy, the God of your understanding bore you up and supported you through your journey. Your continued walk in reclaiming your agency and making right choices is one way you can pay back that loan.

Your progression of agency across this continuum of healing and recovery might be better understood when considering the stages of recovery below:

Early Recovery: Reach out for help—"Please help me."

Middle Recovery: Get through the day—"Help me hold on today."

Later Recovery: Get through the day purposefully— "God, what is your will for me today and how does it fit in the bigger picture of my life?"

With time in recovery, you may be able to plan and think beyond the moment or day and plan for a lifetime and beyond: "God, what is it you want me to be? How can I understand your will and carry it out today, tomorrow, and forever?"

Just as our walk down the continuum of addiction is a process that takes time (for most of us), our walk out of addiction into recovery is a one-day-at-a-time effort that extends over a lifetime. Though we are all taught that recovery is a process that is never-ending, it is only by personal experience that we fully understand the meaning of this statement.

If we allow the pain of life to exceed the resources of

recovery, we put ourselves and our recovery at risk. If we stay in this place for long periods of time, choice can once again become impaired. After twenty-four years of parenting, Sterling experienced this tentative balance between the resources collected over years of recovery and the acute pain that sometimes expresses itself in difficult life circumstances.

🍂 Following a dark and difficult experience where my daughter was hurt very badly, resentment and anger began to dominate my life. Revenge was at the top of my priority list and was fueled by a hurt that only a father in these circumstances could understand. I was consumed with these feelings and felt compelled to fix things by lashing out to satisfy my own desires. Wrapped up in my own pain, I was less able to see the pain my daughter was experiencing and the pain I was inflicting upon the rest of my family. I was aloof, cold, and vindictive. It was all I could do to keep my head above the torrent of emotions that were sweeping through me.

One day while I was preoccupied with working my plan of revenge, I bumped into my daughter as I walked through our living room. She impeded my progress by stepping in front of me to give me a hug, making it impossible to side-step her. I was caught between my daughter, the couch, and the wall. After I gave her a lackluster greeting (something that was normal for me at that dark and desolate time), with tears in her eyes my daughter said something that will stay with me forever. It is a lesson that I will always remember and often share with those in similar circumstances. She took me by the hands, looked in my eyes, and said, "Daddy, if you don't heal from this, none of the rest of us will ever heal from this."

Though her statement was beautifully said and precisely accurate, I didn't want to hear anything about healing or moving on. After all, I had business to attend to that would require a level of anger and hate that I thought could not be tempered by a daughter's plea. In an effort to emotionally run from her request, I looked up to break eye contact and happened to stare right into a big mirror that was hanging on the wall behind where we stood. At that moment I saw my face in the mirror and witnessed the darkness that comes with unresolved rage, sadness, and fear. It seemed as if the conversation went into slow motion and the world ceased to spin on its axis. I was transfixed by the image that I saw and the darkness of the countenance that was staring back at me.

At that moment I realized the extent of my free fall. I could see the fear, the anger, and the pain that had beset me, and I understood what people, most importantly my daughter, had been encountering in their dealings with me. I was a complete mess. My desire to protect my daughter, after the fact, had led me to a selfish conclusion that did nothing to aid her healing or to consider her needs. I was trying to salve my own pain without any consideration as to its impact on others. Sound familiar?

Like the selfishness of addiction, where the addict's pain is paramount and nobody else's needs are considered, I was on a one-man mission that would have more than a one-man impact. Actions that might bring some degree of relief for me would only add to the pain that my daughter and others were already trying to cope with. Her request of me, though initially deflected by the armor of anger and revenge, penetrated deep into my soul. This was the moment when I realized that selfishness was no longer an option, that my healing was a prerequisite for the healing of her and others. I had to find my agency and regain my choice. It was absolutely essential that I find a way to forgive if I was going to help "my little girl" to heal and be well, and if I was going to heal myself.

Despite this revelation, the next few days were very hard—I vacillated back and forth between a need to find forgiveness and a desire to seek revenge. I felt my agency, my ability to make right choices, slipping away. All of my feelings came to a head on a Friday afternoon following our multi-family groups at the treatment facility. Despite my daughter's plea, I had decided on revenge.

Given the nature of this task, I realized that I would need to use in order to accomplish my goal. It is not in my nature to want to be vindictive at such a level. In essence, I had decided to shelve one goal (a lifetime of living recovery principles) to accomplish another (payback or revenge). These decisions were a good indication of how far my agency had slipped—how little attention I had been paying to my spiritual life and to my recovery. Though I couldn't stop thinking about my daughter's plea for healing, I seemed to be propelled down a spiral of retribution. Everyone in my path was going to pay: in my mind, that is what justice demanded.

I will never forget the look on my colleague Tom's face following an angry outburst at another driver on our return home from the treatment facility. I was angry at the person who had cut me off from the lane I was seeking to turn into. At this moment, a beast of monumental proportions came roaring out, a beast I had not seen in many years. I was out of control—I knew it and Tom knew it. I apologized profusely and tried to cover for my indiscretion. However, the cat was out of the bag, and it was clear that I was making choices that looked more like someone active in addiction. On one level I was mortified because of my lack of control. On another level it was nice to share the secret that I was in pain and about to explode. After dropping Tom off, I went home to spend the next couple of painful hours considering my options.

None of the options seemed to offer relief from the pain. I knew that the revenge option would only be a temporary fix—it would be a self-medicating attempt on my part only to have to deal with the wreckage that would eventually emerge from my actions. It would be a quick fix and provide temporary relief in exchange for a lifetime of pain—pain for my family, for my daughter, and for me. Even with the understanding that this was a bad trade, I was still inclined to pursue this path, despite the fear of doing so.

Knowing that I would probably take the low road, and in a last-ditch effort to prevent my free fall, I called my colleague and friend Tom. I asked if I could talk to him—he said, "Sure." He asked when, and I said, "Right now." When asked how soon I could be there, I told him that I was waiting outside his house as we spoke. With no hesitation, my good friend came out of his house and spent the next hour helping me to find my way.

This experience with Tom ended the free fall and began the process of me turning my will back over to God. Turning my will over to God and once again listening to His will for my life allowed me to reestablish my agency and begin to rebuild my recovery lifestyle. The humility that came when I looked up to God propelled me forward to seek and find forgiveness. Reaching out for help from my friend Tom at that key moment was my immediate salvation. Receiving and extending forgiveness would be the key to my long-term healing.

In regard to forgiveness, the receiving part of the equation sounded good, but the extending forgiveness part seemed a tall task for a prideful father from West Texas. I knew God would forgive me. I knew I needed to forgive myself. But I wasn't sure that I was prepared to forgive the person who hurt my daughter. However, it became clear that I could forgive and live, or hold the grudge and die. It would be my choice. Interestingly enough, I began at this point to choose life, not just for me, but for my whole family—especially my sweet daughter.

The next few weeks were spent reading books on forgiveness and communing with my Higher Power. During this time I began to find the miracle of healing that will always come when we tap into the unconditional love and mercy of our Higher Power. My daughter was right. After I found healing, all of us were able to find healing. What a blessed journey this has been! 🐾

When we consider the preceding story from an addiction continuum perspective, it is clear that I had allowed the pain of my family trial to cloud my thinking and impact my choices. Like with a bad infection, my pain increased and I was less able to fight the feelings that infected me. My recovery immune system was compromised, and my will was being hijacked by the pain of revenge and anger. Each day I allowed this hijacking to continue, I slipped further down the continuum of agency and began to lose the choice that I had so carefully developed over the years. As I became more and more emotionally impaired, I became less able to make appropriate choices. I had regressed to a much earlier time in my life, when addiction ruled and the compulsions that accompanied it were king. I was on a path that could have led to relapse, whether it was what I wanted or not. In essence, I had slowly lost my choice in the matter; my only choice was to reach out for help. Thank goodness I did—it was something I have asked others to do as part of their therapeutic regimen for years. At a critical moment, Tom was an important key person for me. Do you have a key person in your life?

One of the common themes of good recovery is learning to lessen, manage, and better cope with the pain of life. Pain, if left unchecked, will rob you of your agency. Pain comes from childhood trauma, unresolved familial issues, mental health disorders (depression, anxiety, attention deficit/hyperactivity disorder, and so on), current stressors, or a whole host of other factors. Pain is part of the addictive spiral and must be resolved, or it could potentially hijack the process, no matter how much time you have in recovery.

Two things must work in concert to maintain good recovery.

First, pain must always be monitored and dealt with appropriately. What you should be monitoring are stressors that can be physical, emotional, familial, occupational, or spiritual in nature. Second, recovery resources should always be considered and adequately stockpiled. Resources are the emotional assets in your life that help you to cope. These resources include spirituality, good relationships, key persons, sponsors, home groups, counselors, and so on. The skill of reaching out to others for help stands alone as one of the most effective of all the coping resources. Collecting resources is like storing food for a famine. You may have more of it than you need at any given time, but you may not have enough if a disaster were to strike. This is where the stressors of life begin to exceed your coping resources, making you vulnerable to additional stress and potential relapse.

As a result, the recovery process should always be assessed based on your level of pain (negative) and your potential recovery resources (positive). As stated earlier in this book, if your stressors exceed your coping resources for long periods of time, the net result will be pain, and pain often comes before relapse. However, good recovery is possible if you build your resources and limit your stressors such that your resources exceed your stress level. Remember, coping with stress and pain more effectively is possible. You do this by limiting your stressors and building your recovery resources. Your biggest recovery resource is found in your recovery relationships and your ability to reach out for help at critical moments.

Considerations of Reclamation of Agency

The progression of the disease narrows choices for the addict and his or her family. At the very end of the addiction spiral, the only choices that remain are to continue to use (engage in addictive behavior) or reach out for help.

- Study the "Journey to Addiction" diagram presented in this chapter. Where do you currently stand on the continuum?

- What is it like to consider that you can reclaim your ability to make good choices one day at a time and change your location on the continuum?

In this chapter, addiction is compared to an eclipse where use blocks out the sunlight of the spirit—your connection with your Higher Power.

- Can you remember the days of darkness?

- In your recovery, have you felt the sunlight of the spirit come through?

- As the eclipse wanes, what choices can you see more clearly?

We refer to "beer goggles," meaning that you have clouded vision as you make the transition from addiction to recovery.

- Are you still looking at life with your beer goggles on?

- Is the cloudiness beginning to fade?

- What would it be like to look at life with a new set of goggles provided by your Higher Power?

The stages of recovery as we see them from early recovery to later recovery are presented in this chapter.

- What stage of recovery are you currently in?

Ask the following questions of your Higher Power and listen for a response:

- "What is your will for me today?"
- "What is it you want me to be?"
- "What is it you want me to become?"

Think back to Sterling's story about pain. You must be ready to deal with life's difficulties and the pain that accompanies them.

- What are the things in your life that continue to be a source of pain for you?
- How are you managing the pain?
- Have you made a commitment to stay in recovery for the long haul, no matter what happens?
- How are you fortifying yourself against the future pain that will certainly come?
- Who are those people you will reach out to for help in your moments of pain?
- What other resources have you stored away to utilize during life's trials and struggles?

• • •

Below are statements to assist in the evaluating of your reclamation of agency. As you consider your choices within the context of these statements, keep in mind that recovery is a day-to-day journey. Reclaiming your choice not to use is an ongoing process. As you consider and apply the concepts outlined in this chapter, you should see your choices more clearly. Seeing and acting on these choices is an outcome of good recovery.

On the scale provided, assess your level of agency or choice based on the following statements:

1	2	3	4	5
Very Low Agency	Low Agency	Middle Agency	High Agency	Very High Agency

I am better able to be responsible
for my choices.   _____

The choices in my life are clear to me.   _____

I see and act upon healthy choices.   _____

I can control my behavior.   _____

My choices have more healthy outcomes.   _____

I am making good choices in my recovery.   _____

▶ If your pattern of answers falls in the middle to high end of the scale, then you are on the right track for today and you are reclaiming your ability to choose.

▶ If you find yourself falling in the middle to low end of the scale, either you are early in recovery and still learning about yourself, or you are struggling and need to reach out for help.

CONCLUSION

Spirituality

As you apply the principles outlined in this book, we believe you will increase your chances at long-term recovery. Additionally, if utilized correctly and daily, these principles will help you to assess the vitality of your recovery at any point along the way. Each principle allows you to evaluate specific areas of strength and/or weakness, enabling you to make important adjustments.

Our discovery and understanding of these principles began in discussions with individuals and families in recovery. After teaching these principles in our multi-family groups, we often ask, "What is missing from these principles?" Inevitably the participants tell us that we forgot to include "spirituality." We agree that the principle of spirituality is missing in the list of six principles. However, we have always understood and taught the six principles within a context of spirituality. We have resisted the urge to include spirituality as one of the six specific principles because, in truth, it is the meta-principle—

the framework or glue that holds the other principles together.

Your spirituality and recovery are best understood as a process that will progressively unfold over your lifetime. As you move forward, your understanding and application of these six principles will shift over time until they become part of your core identity. This process of integration looks something like this.

The beginning of recovery is often referred to as a "moment of clarity" or a "spiritual awakening." In this moment you learn that you must give your will over to your Higher Power. When you experience this awakening, your spiritual journey has begun. There is a reawakening allowing for a renewal of **hope** and the ability to expect good things with greater confidence. This budding connection helps you to realize that you are not such a bad person and you can be forgiven for the mistakes of the past (**identity**). Your Higher Power teaches you that you can **cope** differently—without drugs, alcohol, or other addictive behaviors. This spiritual connection allows you to connect not only to your Higher Power but to others in recovery as well. You see **relationships** in a different light and begin to understand their importance. These efforts propel you toward the **achievement/accomplishment** of small yet important victories. As you move through this process of recovery, your Higher Power provides assurances you can **reclaim** your ability to make right choices. The most important "right choice" is the choice not to use or to engage in addictive behaviors.

As spirituality increases over time, **hope** begins to grow and becomes more embedded and stable. Similarly, your **identity** becomes more positive and immovable and is less affected by moments of pain and fleeting influences. You begin to believe you are a "good person capable of great things." At this point in your spiritual journey, **healthy coping** is more than a suggestion—it becomes a personal desire exercised with consistency. Because of your intimate relationship with your Higher Power, you are better able to **connect** in meaningful ways with those you love. Such a connection is an **achievement and accomplishment** in and of itself. These relationship victories offer both support and added confidence to **achieve** even greater levels of personal, relational, and professional success. Your participation in these processes of recovery allows you to see alternative and more positive **choices (agency)** and to act on them accordingly. When in pain or dealing with stress, you have an expanded ability to make good choices. As stated before, you are able to more confidently make the choice not to use or engage in other addictive behaviors.

Long-term sustained recovery, which includes a trusting and established pattern of spirituality, bears wonderful fruits—one of the amazing blessings of lasting recovery. **Hope** is a present and active principle readily available in your life. When life becomes difficult, you are able to tap into a reservoir of "experience, strength, and hope" obtained through the journey of your recovery and your relationship with your Higher Power. Your **identity** becomes a solid foundation in your life. You love yourself and others by embracing your strengths and accepting your weaknesses. Your spiritual connection is profound, and you see clearly the differences between the person you once were and the person the God of your understanding wants you to become. You have the ability to **cope** effectively with whatever trial comes your way. Because of your ability to cope, you think less of using and more about the goodness of your life in recovery.

Relationships established through the process of recovery are more intimate, meaningful, and trustworthy. They provide you with a "safe place to lay your head" in the storms of life and enable you to provide similar levels of safety for others. As a person who has the capacity to create a safe place for others, you become an asset in your relationships because you give as much as you receive. All of your **achievements** and **accomplishments** are placed within a spiritual framework— they are directed and driven by your Higher Power. Your life has great purpose and meaning: you know who you are and what God wants you to be and do.

With stability and consistency in your recovery, you have a myriad of **choices** that are no longer cloaked in the deceit of addiction. You are clear on what the choices are, as well as the consequences of those choices, and you are more capable of making right decisions. At any given moment, the probability that you will use is very low. You have **reclaimed** enough of your **agency** that you will choose *not* to use or engage in other additive behaviors; however, you have the humility and gratitude to be ever vigilant.

Though you may not identify as an addict or alcoholic, the process of recovery and spiritual growth addressed above is for those who love addicts as well. Recovery is as important for you as it is for the addict. Engaging in the process of recovery as outlined in this book will help you recover from the pain of alcoholism/addiction which comes from being connected to an alcoholic/addict. In applying these six principles, remember to evaluate your own recovery and not the recovery of others.

Your job is to take care of yourself and to function in your primary role. Your role is to be the mother, not the sponsor; the father, not the therapist; the sister or brother, not the treatment professional; the friend, not the community support group. Specific recovery help is best provided by persons who are more objective and experienced in the recovery journey. As you focus on yourself and your efforts within your primary role, you give your loved ones the best chance at recovery success, and yourself the best chance at reclaiming your own life.

Whether alcoholic, addict, family member, or friend, your spiritual life must be continually nurtured. We recommend you incorporate service as a key way to foster your recovery and spiritual wellness. These activities can be as simple as small personal acts of service, service projects, and/or longer-term service endeavors. It is not so important how big or small the project is, but the consistency in which you offer yourself to be helpful. Service provides a constant check on your level of pride. Your service will help you maintain humility, increase gratitude, and expand your capacity to remain connected to your Higher Power.

With humility you are better able to engage in the "searching and fearless moral inventory" required in the Twelve Steps. As you work your program, you understand the need for forgiveness in your life, the kind of forgiveness and acceptance gifted to you by your Higher Power in Steps One through Three. Our experience tells us that, in some cases, it is harder for an addict (or a family member) to forgive him- or herself than to forgive others. Though still difficult, making amends to others is often the more direct and easier thing to accomplish.

Early in your recovery walk, the relationship forged with your Higher Power provides insight as to why you are worthy of forgiveness, despite the wreckage of your past. In the beginning, your Higher Power extended an unconditional love and acceptance because you were worthy of such love and acceptance. If your Higher Power believes you are worth loving, then you must believe you are loveable and able to be forgiven. If the God of your understanding graciously gives you the gift of forgiveness and love, you must graciously accept it in return. As author and ethicist Lewis B. Smedes states, "To forgive is to set a prisoner free and discover that the prisoner was you!"

When you fail to forgive yourself, you remain incarcerated by your past. The love and forgiveness extended by your Higher Power will set you free, but you must first accept the gift.

Although less important, you will find that many of those you make amends to will offer you their forgiveness and support. Their ability to extend this forgiveness should further highlight your acceptability, despite past mistakes and current imperfections. When people do not accept your amends, it is important that you consider that their inability to forgive is part of their own spiritual journey and not a commentary on your worth or recovery. It is imperative that you not see forgiveness as the option of the weak, but a quality of the strong. This message is clear in a quote from Mahatma Gandhi: "The weak can never forgive. Forgiveness is the attribute of the strong."

Given the gift you have received from your Higher Power and others, you have an obligation and responsibility to extend the same mercy to others. This extension of mercy is a process and often takes considerable effort over an extended period of time. Sterling's experience with his daughter and the need to extend forgiveness to someone who had hurt her highlights the difficulty of this process of forgiveness. It also highlights that forgiveness is possible and yields remarkable outcomes. In a critical moment, Sterling came across a quote that offered him profound guidance and motivation to find and practice the principle of forgiveness. The quote is as follows:

Forgiveness is freeing up and putting to better use the energy once consumed by holding grudges, harboring resentments, and nursing unhealed wounds. It is rediscovering the strengths we always had and relocating our limitless capacity to understand and accept other people and ourselves.

— DR. SIDNEY SIMON, *FORGIVENESS*

As we are strengthened by the process of recovery, we become forgiveness capable. Consideration regarding the forgiving of yourself, making amends, and forgiving others should be part of your daily spiritual walk.

One way you can engage in the process of forgiveness and evaluate your spiritual wellness is through prayer and meditation. Regular and consistent prayer removes the ceiling between you and your Higher Power, keeping open a conduit of communication. Meditation takes prayer to the next level, allowing you to receive personal inspiration regarding your communication with God and all other aspects of your life. It brings a calming influence that allows you to determine your connection with your Higher Power and your level of confidence in that connection. This confidence is reflected in your peace, your serenity, and your ability to be still—the fruits of prayer and meditation. Though prayer and meditation require you to slow down, the result helps you to clarify the "next right thing to do" in your life. Prayer and meditation must be supplemented by exploring recovery literature, holy writings, and/or other good books.

As discussed in the introduction, we offer the recovery prayer as a way to solidify the principles taught in this book and bring you closer to your Higher Power.

God, thank you for the chance at recovery.

Grant me **hope** and transform me into a new person who can **cope** more effectively.

Help me recognize the **accomplishments** in my life and develop a greater **capacity for meaningful relationships.**

As I emerge anew, **change my identity** to one more positive and allow me to reclaim my **agency** by always choosing recovery.

Amen.

Your renewed relationship with your Higher Power should provide a foundation for establishing the other relationships in your life. Characteristics of your relationship with your Higher Power should be found in your important attachments. These include unconditional love and acceptance, mercy, forgiveness, understanding, support, equity, fairness, and—above all—safety. As you grow in this connection, you will begin to understand how these characteristics can be realized in your daily interactions. We encourage you to model every relationship in your recovery after your relationship with your Higher Power.

Among people in recovery, relapse is the most difficult "R" to discuss—nobody wants to talk about relapse. Relapse is defined not as a punctuated point in time, but as a process of falling out of recovery. The outcome of this process is a return to use or other addictive behaviors. If you are fortunate enough to survive this process of relapse (and it is a risk), please remember that it doesn't have to be the end of your recovery nor do you return to a place of "zero" recovery. However, the longer you stay in relapse, the harder it is to find the other "R": recovery. The longer you continue to use after a relapse, the more you will erode your hard-earned agency or choice.

What you did in the beginning of your recovery journey can be reinstituted here. Reach out for help first to your Higher Power and then to others. Don't let the shame and guilt of relapse prevent you from reaching out and moving forward. Even in relapse, your Higher Power is willing and able to receive you. So are the key persons in your life and others who understand recovery and are willing to help without judgment. That said, there are many who reach out for help in their addiction, enter recovery, and never relapse. By assessing your recovery one day at a time, utilizing the Twelve Steps, working a recovery program, evaluating your walk based on the six principles in this book, and monitoring your spirituality, you have a great opportunity to experience the joy of lasting recovery.

Considerations of Spirituality

As stated earlier, the beginning of recovery is often referred to as a "moment of clarity" or a "spiritual awakening." Recovery is best begun with spirituality at its foundation. Spirituality also provides the context that allows recovery to become a lifelong process.

Consider the role that spirituality has played in your life and in your recovery.

- How can a spiritual focus benefit you in your recovery?

- Compare and contrast the difference in your level of

spirituality in your addiction, in your initial step into recovery, and currently.

This chapter discusses the process of growth in recovery related to the six principles. In this presentation, we talk about the beginning, middle, and later parts of recovery.

- Where are you in your level of growth related to these six principles? What is your level of progress?
- Are you early in your recovery, are you in the middle part, or have you been in recovery a long time?
- How is spirituality related to your progress and your understanding of these six principles?

Remember, family members, you should assess your own growth related to these principles and not the growth of your recovering loved one.

- Family member: Are you playing the role (mother, father, son, daughter, brother, and so on) you were intended to play within your family?
- How can you free yourself from the need to play other roles meant for sponsors, therapists, and home group members?
- How can your own spirituality, your recovery, and the six principles discussed in this book help you to let go and begin trusting your Higher Power?

Service is a key component to lasting recovery and heightened spiritual awareness. In addition, service fosters greater levels of humility. Evaluate the level of service you are currently offering.

- What role has service played in your recovery?
- What types of service opportunities are you engaging in?
- Are there additional opportunities you can take advantage of?

Forgiveness is another key component to recovery and spirituality.

- Have you experienced love and forgiveness in your relationship with your Higher Power? If not, what can you do differently to experience this love and forgiveness?
- Are you able to extend love and forgiveness to yourself and others? If not, how can continuing to apply the six principles help you in this journey?
- How can you model the unconditional love and acceptance you received from your Higher Power for yourself and others?
- How does the kind of forgiveness and redemption received from your Higher Power help you in making amends?

Prayer and meditation are important in nurturing spiritual wellness. Assess yourself in your ability to connect with your Higher Power through prayer and meditation.

- Have you considered combining prayer and meditation?
- How would combining these two important activities assist in your spiritual journey?
- What does the "ability to be still" referred to in this chapter mean to you?
- Have you experienced the "stillness" that results from prayer and meditation?

Though a reality for some, relapse is an unpopular notion among recovering addicts and their family members.

- How can your spirituality be utilized to prevent relapse?
- If you relapse, how can your spirituality make a difference in what you do next?

Remember, even in relapse, your Higher Power and many others are waiting to assist you as you move forward in your recovery journey.

- Are you able to see that no matter what you do, your Higher Power will not abandon you?

References

AA World Services. 2002. *Alcoholics Anonymous,* 4th ed. New York: Alcoholics Anonymous World Services, Inc.

Brown, S., and V. Lewis. 1999. *The Alcoholic Family in Recovery: A Developmental Model.* New York: Guilford Press.

Gottman, J. M., and N. Silver. 2004. *The Seven Principles for Making Marriage Work: A Practical Guide from the Country's Foremost Relationship Expert.* New York: Random House.

Shumway, S. T., T. G. Kimball, J. B. Dakin, K. S. Harris, and A. K. Baker. 2011. "Multi-Family Groups in Recovery: A Revised Multi-Family Curriculum." *The Journal of Family Psychotherapy* 22: 1–18.

Shumway, S. T., and R. S. Wampler. 2002. "A Behaviorally Focused Measure for Relationships: The Couple Behavior Report (CBR)." *The American Journal of Family Therapy* 30: 311–321.

Wegscheider-Cruse, S. 1981. *Another Chance: Hope and Health for the Alcoholic Family*. Palo Alto, CA: Science and Behavioral Books.

About the Authors

Thomas G. Kimball, Ph.D., L.M.F.T. is an associate professor at Texas Tech University and the associate managing director for the Center for the Study of Addiction and Recovery. He teaches family dynamics of addiction at both the undergraduate and the graduate levels. In addition, he is the clinical director of the outpatient program and co-facilitates multi-family groups at The Ranch at Dove Tree— an inpatient alcohol and drug treatment program. Tom has been married to his wife, Melissa, for twenty years and has five children.

Sterling T. Shumway, Ph.D., L.M.F.T. is a regents' professor in the Department of Applied and Professional Studies, Addictive Disorders and Recovery Studies Division (ADRS) at Texas Tech University. He currently serves as the program director of the Addiction and Recovery Studies Program. In addition, he has a private therapy practice where he sees individuals, couples, and families and also co-facilitates multi-family groups as the family program director at The Ranch at Dove Tree. Sterling has been married to his wife, Valerie, for twenty-nine years and has five children and three grandchildren.

The Ranch at Dove Tree provides detoxification, residential (including a special collegiate residential track), sober living, and intensive outpatient services to individuals seeking help for substance dependency. Located on ranchland just north of Lubbock, Texas, this fifty-six-bed facility specializes in working with both the client and family in the recovery process. See and learn more at ranchatdovetree.com.

Hazelden, a national nonprofit organization founded in 1949, helps people reclaim their lives from the disease of addiction. Built on decades of knowledge and experience, Hazelden offers a comprehensive approach to addiction that addresses the full range of patient, family, and professional needs, including treatment and continuing care for youth and adults, research, higher learning, public education and advocacy, and publishing.

A life of recovery is lived "one day at a time." Hazelden publications, both educational and inspirational, support and strengthen lifelong recovery. In 1954, Hazelden published *Twenty-Four Hours a Day,* the first daily meditation book for recovering alcoholics, and Hazelden continues to publish works to inspire and guide individuals in treatment and recovery, and their loved ones. Professionals who work to prevent and treat addiction also turn to Hazelden for evidence-based curricula, informational materials, and videos for use in schools, treatment programs, and correctional programs.

Through published works, Hazelden extends the reach of hope, encouragement, help, and support to individuals, families, and communities affected by addiction and related issues.

For questions about Hazelden publications,
please call **800-328-9000**
or visit us online at **hazelden.org/bookstore**.